THE
JOYCHIEVER
JOURNEY

JAMES
HOUSE
M E D I A

www.jameshousemedia.co

ISBN: 978-0-578-74837-5 (print)

ISBN: 978-0-578-74838-2 (ebook)

Ordering Information:

For large quantity purchases by corporations, associations, and others, please contact www.jameshousemedia.co.

TABLE OF CONTENTS

THE JOYCHIEVER JOURNEY

EVADE BURNOUT, SURPASS YOUR GOALS AND OUT-HAPPY EVERYONE

TRACY LALONDE

PROLOGUE

From one overachiever to another, let me ask you: Are you as happy, fulfilled, and aligned with joy as you could be?

Let me tell you a story about Lauren, who did everything right.

Lauren is the only child of an upper-middle-class family. Her parents work hard to be able to provide a comfortable home and lifestyle. They have successful careers, which means they can take the family on nice vacations every year, splurge on a nice car, and shop at the trendy clothes stores.

They want the same for Lauren.

In first grade, Lauren receives her first ever report card. She has all E's, which in her school system are the equivalent of A's. Her father, however, thinks that the E's are F's. He lectures her to tears about the importance of good grades before her mother steps in and clarifies the situation.

Though Lauren knows that her father misunderstands, she feels terrible and never wants to disappoint him again.

This is the beginning of the road on Lauren's overachiever journey.

Lauren does very well in school, both academically and in extra-curricular activities. She gets top marks and graduates as valedictorian. She is captain of the basketball team during her junior and senior years and is on the Homecoming Court. She becomes president of her school's National Honor Society and competes at the state level in math competitions.

Everyone is proud of her—parents, teachers, and coaches—and Lauren is proud of herself. She likes being on top, popular, and successful.

She has put in a tremendous amount of hard work to attain those achievements.

Lauren performs well at university. She secures good grades, joins a sorority, volunteers on campus, and holds leadership positions. Lauren lands a great job after college that sends her traveling throughout the US. It's exciting, fun, and exhausting all at the same time. She meets all types of people, develops her communication skills, and has experiences she could have never dreamed of having. Lauren has continued success in her career and becomes a co-owner of a small consulting company in her 30's.

She perceives herself to be incredibly successful.

As a consultant, she is flourishing. She has an amazing personal brand and reputation in her business sector, has more clients than she could have hoped for, and is doing very well financially. Her company is in high demand. She is one of its stars. And she feels on top of the world.

Life is fantastic…until it isn't.

In her mid-40's, after ten years with her company and seemingly at the pinnacle of her career, Lauren unexpectedly leaves the business.

Lauren's journey represents that of many overachievers. It begins with others frequently telling them what they expect. Over time, overachievers internalize those expectations and make them their own. Get good grades. Select a major. Graduate from college. Get a job. Succeed. Earn more money. Buy more things. Move up in the organization. Complete the next project. Gain the boss' attention and approval. Become a boss. Retire. Die.

Now please understand. There is nothing wrong with this process on its surface. But for many, it isn't tied to meaning, purpose, or joy, and some might even be suffocating from the weight of it all.

That was Lauren.

Is this you? Does it reflect aspects of your life?

It was me. I am Lauren.

This is my story and what led me to realize that I had to change my life. I *had* to focus more on joy.

On paper, my life sounded fantastic, but there is a dark side to the journey you just read about. I was on the road 40 weeks a year, often in three cities a week. It wasn't uncommon for me to take up to nine flights a week. I often stayed in hotels for over 100 nights a year. I prided myself on my high-flying status with airlines and hotels. My phone was attached to my body, and 12-hour days were my norm.

When I did get home, all I ever thought about was work, and I'd spend Sunday afternoons preparing for the next week. Forget about hobbies, charities, or friends. I didn't have time. I wasn't reliable socially as I often couldn't attend whatever gathering or dinner I was invited to or had to cancel at short notice. Eventually, people just stopped inviting me and friendships floundered. I gained weight, my hair thinned, and I began having heart palpitations from the stress.

I became a hostage to work. How often do you feel captive to work?

So yes, I achieved so much but I had little joy in my life. I was incredibly conflicted: I relished my work and my clients, I utilized my strengths almost daily, I had great success, and I loved the euphoria that came with meeting a challenge. But I was exhausted. My lifestyle and drive to perform was killing me.

For me, this life was unsustainable.

Does this sound familiar? Is the way *you're* living unsustainable?

After I left that company in my 40's, I started my own consulting business and have continued to help clients find the best versions of themselves. For over 20 years, I have taught and coached lawyers at major corporate law firms primarily on business development, public speaking, and communication skills. I work with incredibly smart and successful people every day who show the telltale signs of overachieving.

Through my coaching, I regularly have conversations with individuals who don't have enough hours in the day, feel pulled in a number of directions professionally and personally, and feel like they're continuously letting themselves and their families down. They struggle to feel like they're living up to expectations, let alone find "extra" time for joy.

With their experiences and mine, I have been inspired to find another way of living…for myself, for them, and for you. You can be wildly successful AND have a joy-filled life, and this book will provide the roadmap.

EVADING BURNOUT – THE OVERACHIEVER'S CHALLENGE

"Achievement brings its own anticlimax."

— Maya Angelou

Each overachiever's path is unique, but we all share many of the same characteristics:

- Parents, teachers, and society set expectations for us.
- Eventually we create the same expectations for ourselves.
- We focus on what it takes to get to the "top," and we want it NOW.
- We work hard to achieve and take pride in the sweat.
- We continuously push to the next level.
- We get caught in a continuous cycle of comparison to successful people.
- We strive to leapfrog over others to get to the top.
- We spend little time enjoying our achievements as we quickly analyze what we could have done better and set our sights on the next rung.
- We outwork everyone else. We arrive early, stay late, and respond to emails within minutes at all hours of the day,

every day of the week.

- We are infrequently impressed with our own accomplishments or how far we have come.
- We leave little time for ourselves.
- We give up significant aspects of our personal lives to be successful.
- Our relationships often suffer as they take a backseat to work.
- We live lives that are stressful, frenetic, and often empty of meaning.
- We rarely pause long enough to see if we are TRULY happy.

Overachiever's Formula for Success

Many overachievers believe that you must have success before you can have happiness. It is beat into our brains that all the hard work will pay off, even if the work itself isn't fun. That's why it's called work.

When you look up "hard work" in a thesaurus, other words or phrases that appear are grind, long haul, uphill struggle, drudgery, and backbreaking. None of that sounds like any fun, which is a bummer because work comprises 50%–58% of your waking hours on any given workday.

Yet work is an enormous part of an overachiever's formula for success.

We also place a huge emphasis on having a strong "work ethic." BusinessDictionary.com describes work ethic as "the belief that work has a moral benefit and an inherent ability to strengthen character." It implies that if you don't have a good work ethic that you are somehow a lesser human being.

"Hard work" and "work ethic" have become standards by which overachievers measure themselves. Working a crazy number of hours—50–60+ hours a week—and sacrificing self and relationships are the norm. On top of that, according to a Gallup Study in 2018 of 7,500 full-time employees, 67% experienced burnout.[i]

Productivity, dedication, discipline, determination, and perseverance are important characteristics for accomplishing goals, but the real challenge overachievers have is this:

They often lose sight of the meaning or purpose for the sacrifice and rarely enjoy the journey while they are on it.

Overachievers certainly enjoy moments along the journey, but generally, it can feel like a grind. Overachievers often fall victim to what I call the "Once I…" syndrome. Once I work hard enough to get the right job, get promoted, get the kids into college, make enough money, or retire, *THEN* I can have fun or enjoy my life.

An overachiever's formula for success often looks like:

EFFORT	+	ATTAINMENT	+	RECOGNITION	=	**SUCCESS**
Studying		Grades		Praise		
Practicing		Wins		Awards		
Hard work		University		Reputation		
Late nights		Great job		Money		
Sacrifice		Promotions		Titles		

Success comes after everything else. The concept of "I made it" always seems elusive. And heaven forbid that we don't get to the top. As the popular saying goes, "Second place is the first loser."

There CAN be another way. In fact, it is imperative that there MUST be another way. Otherwise, we will all die an early death or have many regrets when the end does come, as Bronnie Ware discovered.

A palliative care nurse, Bronnie Ware, asked her dying patients over an eight-year period what regrets they had. Her work culminated in a blog and then a book called *The Top Five Regrets of Dying.* You may have heard these regrets before, but they're worth repeating here.

1. I wish I'd had the courage to live a life true to myself, not the life others expected of me.
2. I wish I hadn't worked so hard.
3. I wish I'd had the courage to express my feelings.
4. I wish I had stayed in touch with my friends.
5. I wish that I had let myself be happier.

Are you feeling any of these regrets now, at this point in your life?

Ware says that not having the courage to live a life true to oneself is the most common regret. "When people realize that their life is almost over and look back clearly on it, it's easy to see *how many dreams have gone unfulfilled.* Most people had not honored even a half of their dreams and had to die knowing that it was due to choices they had made, or not made."[ii]

Once we are on the overachiever path, it's hard to veer from it.

The overachiever path does have its benefits, but often we get trapped in those benefits or stuck in this way of life. It becomes virtually impossible to:

- Envision a different kind of life for ourselves.
- Ignore others' expectations of us.
- Support our families financially by following any other path.

You have, no doubt, heard stories of people who have left the "corporate" life and opened a winery in Tuscany or bought a cute B&B on a Caribbean island. It seems too idyllic to even be a real possibility. It feels like a dream, and one that you can't even contemplate. But, boy, wouldn't it be nice?

Now I'm not suggesting that you have to chuck it all and make such a dramatic change in order to find more joy. The problem, however, is that even if you have another viable option or path that you could pursue, one that could support a financially secure lifestyle and provide more joy, you usually dismiss it. You somehow acquire a "learned helplessness" that prevents you from contemplating *any* change to improve the joy factor in your life.

Learned helplessness was first discovered by Martin Seligman and Steven Maier in the late 1960's and early 1970's. In their study, the researchers would ring a bell and then give a light shock to two groups of dogs. One group could stop the shock by pressing a button with their noses. The second group had no such button and no way to stop it. They had to endure the shock.

After a number of rounds, the researchers only rang the bell but did not administer the shock. However, dogs in both groups reacted as if they had been shocked. One group pressed the shock-stopping button, and the second group simply waited to receive the shock.

In the second part of the experiment, the dogs in both groups had the option to avoid the shock by simply jumping over a low fence. Upon administering the shock, the first group of dogs quickly jumped over the fence. However, the second group did not leap to safety. They lay down and took the shock. It was as though they had learned from the first part of the experiment that they couldn't avoid the shock, so they simply gave in and withstood it.[iii]

Overachievers often aren't so different from the dogs in the second group of this study. When we think we can't do anything to alter the path we're on, we often don't even try to change our circumstances.

The dark side of overachieving—feeling stuck, stressed, exhausted, anxious, and depressed—feels like our destiny. We don't attempt to live another way until we experience significant physical or mental health issues, which forces us to make a change before it kills us.

Consider your life. If you're:

- Wondering why life feels like a non-stop parade of accomplishments;
- Beginning to doubt the accuracy of the success formula you've followed diligently for years;
- Questioning if all the effort is worth the infrequent, fleeting glimpses of contentment;
- Hoping there's more to life than non-stop activity filled with stress, anxiety, and worry;

Then this book is for you.

Believe it or not, it is possible to find joy while still achieving AND enjoy the journey along the way.

Theoretically, we all know that we only have one life, but many of us don't intentionally live that life to **capture as much joy as possible**. We have allowed ourselves to get stuck in a life driven by achievement and accomplishment and we don't seek to discover our true selves to understand how we can be joyful.

Whether you believe it or not, life IS passing you by…and quickly!

Now is the time to be different. What could your life be like if you applied all your positive overachiever skills to aim for joy—just as voraciously as you've aimed for success in the past?

Endnotes

i   Agrawal, Sangeeta and Ben Wigert. "Employee Burnout, Part 1: The 5 Main Causes." Gallup.com. May 14, 2020. Accessed July 03, 2020. https://www.gallup.com/workplace/237059/employee-burnout-part-main-causes.aspx.

ii   Evolution, Collective. "The Top 5 Regrets Of The Dying." *HuffPost*. August 03, 2013. Accessed March 02, 2020. https://www.huffpost.com/entry/top-5-regrets-of-the-dying_n_3640593.

iii   Ackerman, Courtney. "Learned Helplessness: Seligman's Theory of Depression (+ Cure)." PositivePsychology.com. May 12, 2020. Accessed March 03, 2020. https://positivepsychology.com/learned-helplessness-seligman-theory-depression-cure/.

FROM THE PLATEAU OF SUCCESS TO THE PEAK OF HAPPINESS

"Happiness depends upon ourselves."

— *Aristotle*

What is Joy?

It may surprise you to know that the study of joy, known as positive psychology, began relatively recently, in 1998. It was pioneered by the American psychologist, Martin Seligman. Comparatively, conventional psychology, which focuses primarily on dysfunction and abnormalities, started in the late 1800's. Even though positive psychology is a relatively young area of science, many scientists and psychologists have a variety of definitions of what they believe happiness is or comprises. For example:

- Martin Seligman, Director of the Penn Positive Psychology Center, breaks it down into three measurable components: pleasure, engagement, and meaning.[i]

- Tal Ben-Shahar, who created Harvard's most popular course on happiness, finds that a happy person enjoys positive emotions while perceiving his or her life as purposeful. The definition does not pertain to a single moment but to a generalized aggregate of one's experiences.[ii]

- Sonja Lyubomirsky, professor of psychology at the University of California, Riverside, believes happiness is the experience of joy, contentment, and well-being combined with a sense that life is good and worthwhile.[iii]

With all these definitions, one that most resonates with me is the term Aristotle used for happiness—*eudaimonia*. Eudaimonia does not directly translate to "happiness" but rather to "human flourishing."[iv]

I don't know about you, but I want to flourish, rather than simply live. What is the point of doing all the work if you can't flourish? As Kevin Horsley says in his book, *The Happy Mind,* "happiness is the byproduct of a million small things—whether actions, thoughts, or choices—habitually repeated, in an integrated way of living, adding up to a lifetime experience of inner wellbeing."[v]

"Actions, thoughts, or choices—habitually repeated." Think about it. Being joyful is totally up to you. But you do have to work for it, much like anything else that is good in life. You have to seek it out, rather than rely on it to magically happen or fall into your lap. Joy is an active, daily, and intentional choice.

Let me pause here for a moment to discuss the difference between joy and happiness. I have used, and will continue to use, the two terms interchangeably because they are so closely related. In fact, the definition for each has the word of the other within it.

Likewise, when I have asked friends to compare and contrast the two emotions, we struggle to create independent definitions. Yet our conversations have concluded that they *feel* different. Joy feels "happier" or more elevated somehow. So for our exploratory purposes and the journey of life, let's say that joy is the ultimate goal.

Why Joy?

Scientific studies have shown that happy people:

- Are healthier
- Have better mental health
- Are more likely to attract a love partner
- Enjoy stronger and more satisfying marriages
- Are better parents
- Experience greater resilience
- Have an increased capacity to deal with adversity and trauma

Shawn Achor, in his book, *The Happiness Advantage,* discusses a "meta-analysis"[vi] study that compiled over 200 studies on 275,000 people worldwide. The findings reveal that happiness leads to success in nearly every domain, including work, health, friendship, sociability, creativity, and energy. Another meta-analysis of 35 studies[vii] concludes that happy people can live up to 18% longer than their less happy peers. With the current average life expectancy in the US being approximately 72, joy could potentially add 13 years to your life.

Happy people are also good for business. Numerous studies show that happiness creates higher levels of productivity, higher sales, better leaders, higher performance ratings, and higher pay.[viii] In fact, studies show that higher income is more directly related to one's level of happiness than to one's level of education.[ix] Happy workers are also more loyal to the company, take fewer sick days, have fewer conflicts with coworkers, quit their jobs less frequently, and generate greater customer satisfaction.

Alright, I'm in! Where do I sign up? How do I get me some joy?

Finding Your True Self

Towards the end of my "Lauren" run, I literally felt continuously out of breath because I crammed work into every moment of my day. I had so many back-to-back meetings and workshops with clients, it was hard to find time to use the bathroom. I returned phone calls while in cabs from one meeting to another and responded to email for two to three hours each night. I cried every weekend from the weight of all the stress—and it just wasn't fun anymore.

When I left my company burned out, fried, and completely devoid of joy, I tattooed the word "Joy" onto my wrist and told my friends, clients, and colleagues that I was going on a "Joy Journey." I took eight months off to recover, heal, and reclaim my joy.

During this time, I confirmed that I *have* to choose for *me*. Joy is my responsibility. No amount of money, success or other accomplishments or accolades are a substitute for joy. My life needs to be a journey with time to focus on the happy moments rather than a quest for continuous winning. I knew that joy needed to be a regular pursuit and that it doesn't just happen. I had no idea how to behave differently than I had in my overachieving past, but I knew I wanted to find a way.

Let me ask you:

- Have you ever stopped to think about *what you truly want out of your life?*
- Have you ever identified *what makes you happy?*
- Do you even know *what joy feels like on a daily basis,* aside from those moments such as childbirth, marriage, or amazing vacations?
- Do you think it is *possible to achieve and feel joy regularly?*
- If you made the choice for joy, *would you know where to begin?*

What I think happens with overachievers is that you get consumed with the checklist—created by you and often influenced by others—of what you are supposed to do in life. Right university—check! Right job—check! Hard work—check! Advancement—check! And so on. You expend all your energy and effort perpetually reaching, striving for, and achieving the next level. Then at some point, you pause and wonder, "How did I get here? Am I happy?"

It's perplexing, and I believe that one of the reasons is because you don't have a deep enough understanding of self, or what I call your True Self. There are a few reasons why this may be the case. Perhaps you:

- Have never taken the time to explore the inner workings of what makes you tick.
- Have had some clarity at some point but put it aside or have forgotten about it along the way.
- Have embarked on training programs that may have exposed you to certain aspects of yourself, such as personality assessments, leadership styles, etc., but haven't experienced any program that is comprehensive.
- Think this is all a bunch of nonsense—"New-age" mumbo jumbo—and would never bother to explore yourself in this way.

If the fourth bullet resonates with you, then you can stop reading and gift this book to someone who needs it. For the rest of you, please continue on.

Personally, I thought I knew a lot about myself. Over the years, I had identified my strengths and used them regularly. I became clear about my values and considered them when I made important decisions. I was a regular exerciser, ate well, and focused on my health. However, I have since learned that there are more areas to consider and deeper levels of clarity available to me.

During my "Joy Journey" and since, I have been on a continuous hunt to find and dive deeper to discover my True Self. This book is a culmination of those efforts. It offers you an expedited path through all of that learning to help you find YOUR True Self.

Even if you think you have done the work, there is more for you to explore.

My wish for you is that you discover your unique path so you can live with joy routinely. When you can live a life that is expressly yours, joy will follow. Living with joy is about enjoying this moment. It's about waking up, feeling excited to be alive, and feeling grateful to be doing what you're doing. You jump out of bed energized and ready to tackle the day. Your life isn't devoid of problems, but you have the attitude and tools to enjoy the good times and manage the challenging moments.

Becoming a Joychiever

As overachievers, we have developed so many valuable skills over time. We have learned how to set goals and attain them. We practice discipline and work hard to propel ourselves forward. We are motivated to learn and grow skills, and often express patience while developing mastery. We can make tough decisions when required.

What if we applied these skills to the pursuit of joy? Imagine if you applied the same level of overachieving energy and effort to seeking joy.

Rather than being an "overachiever," could you become a "Joychiever?"

- What could your life look like?

- How would you invest your available moments?
- With whom would you spend your time?
- At the end of every day, how many minutes of joy could you claim to have had?

Transforming from an overachiever to a Joychiever is totally doable. Incredible as it may seem, you have it within you right now to make the shift. If you're wondering where to begin, start with the Joychiever Credo.

Joychiever Credo

Here are 10 tenets that Joychievers live by:

- Seek joy as a passionate journey.
- Encourage others to seek joy.
- Refuse to live by chance and postpone joy until after success.
- View the world with positivity.
- Have a clear set of values that guide their decisions.
- Play to their strengths in specific contexts.
- Engage in leisure or hobbies to complement their work lives.
- Make physical health a critical priority.
- Deliberately nurture joy-inducing relationships in all areas of their lives.
- Take moments for themselves on a frequent basis.

It may take effort and time, but as an overachiever, you already know how to set your sights on a goal and work to achieve it. Let's make joychieving your goal!

The Joychiever Journey

I loved those months that I took off to focus on reclaiming my joy.

Who wouldn't? I explored Thailand and China with my husband. We went to a wedding on a beach in Brazil. We saw our dear friends in Lake Como, Italy, where we had gotten married.

I hiked the mountains in Canada and ate lunch at my favorite café afterwards. I read numerous books and exercised most days. I cooked up a storm and had long, leisurely conversations with my family and friends. And I planned my next business venture.

What I have realized now is that if I had gained more clarity about my True Self earlier, maybe I wouldn't have had to unplug or disconnect like I had.

If I had kept some boundaries around work and the associated travel, maybe I could have avoided burnout and the feelings of constantly being in a pressure cooker. I might have felt like I had control over my own life. I could have directed the positive aspects of overachieving towards joy in a manageable way.

Plus, leaving gainful employment for a few months isn't a feasible option for most people. It's just not realistic. But seeking joy IS available to you, no matter where you are in your life. I would like you to join me on the Joychiever Journey: this book lays out the roadmap for your expedition.

The Joychiever's "Happy Place"

The journey begins with figuring out your "Happy Place." This is meant more figuratively than literally, but first, consider how you feel when you are in a joyful state.

For me, I feel a lively happiness. I feel contentment and confidence. I feel gratitude and love. I am relaxed but have calm energy. I smile and laugh easily. There is a spring to my step. I love exploring and discovering new things. I feel alignment with all parts of myself, and I leave time to take in and relish all of the good moments.

Now focus on the physical details of your happy place. If you're not sure what they could be, think about some of the vacations you have taken. We tend to be drawn to the places that make us feel good.

My happy place always involves water. I like to see it, and I like to hear it. It could be a deep blue ocean, a placid lake or a babbling brook. I like to hear the lapping of the waves, watch the ripples from a stream, or witness the power of a waterfall. The sun is shining, and the sky is a brilliant blue. It's perfectly warm, and I can stay outside for hours without sweating or getting burned from the sun. When I try to meditate, these types of scenes are often in my head.

What is your Happy Place? How does it make you feel and what does it look like in your head? Pause for a moment; close your eyes and try to picture it.

As overachievers, we need to have a goal in mind. So for Joychievers, your Happy Place is your *goal*. Whether you can actually visit your Happy Place or not, it is the "destination" where you feel the most joy.

True Self Stops

Like any road trip or trek, you make stops along the way to fuel up, eat, and refresh. For the Joychiever Journey, these "stops" are the places where you will spend time to think, explore, and reflect, which will help you find your True Self. The next seven chapters are your guides for each stop.

If this is the first time that you have done this kind of work, I suggest that you "stop" in each of these locations in the order that they are presented. If you already have clarity in one or more of these areas, then visit the stops that need most attention in your life. The goal is to gain clarity of your True Self so that you can regularly access your Joychiever Happy Place.

However, please remember that life is fluid. Chosen or unexpected changes happen that may prompt you to revisit these stops throughout your life. If you add to your family, for example, you may revisit Values Village and adjust your values. If you have a health issue, you may spend time on Body Beach to heal. If you retire, you may explore Leisure Cove to find how you want to spend your time. The goal is to continuously focus on your True Self throughout your life to maximize joy.

Here are the True Self Stops that will help you reach your Joychiever Happy Place:

1. **Perceptions Vista** – How you take in, or perceive, the world has an enormous impact on happiness. Do you see the glass as half-empty or half-full? Do you look for the positive or the negative first? Do you know that it is possible to rewire your brain towards the positive?

2. **Values Village** – Values are the beliefs that drive every decision you make, and many of you will have never taken the time to clearly define your top priority values. Without this, you are living your life rudderless.

3. **Strengths Mountain** – In our work lives, many over-achievers have gained clarity about their strengths. However, deeper levels of clarity are possible, and the context in which you use those strengths matters—a lot.

4. **Leisure Cove** – It's important to have something to care about that is authentic to you outside of work and separate from family. You need other areas to invest your energy in that bring you joy. It could look like a passion, a hobby, or altruism.

5. **Body Beach** – Without a healthy, functioning body, there is no life, no journey. While there are multiple industries that focus on the body and health, this book focuses on three key aspects that are critical for finding joy: stress, exercise, and sleep.

6. **Relationships Harbor** – Studies have shown that relationships and socialization are critical components to happiness and aging well. You may put a lot of effort into finding a compatible love partner(s), but do you also exert that kind of energy for other relationships in your life? As part of your journey, it's important to examine which of your relationships are joy-inducing as compared to joy-robbing and what to do about those relationships that aren't joyful.

7. **ME Moments Market** – Even when the previous six areas are clear and aligned, you still may not be taking enough time for yourself. You pour yourself into everyone else— either because you have to or because you want to. But taking time for YOU is a critical piece of the Joychiever Journey. In fact, it's mandatory, so we will explore ways that you can fill your personal joy tank, even in the small moments.

Know that reading this book doesn't automatically produce joy. Finding your True Self takes effort. I give you permission to take time to focus just on you. Hopefully, you will enjoy and gain as much from this journey as I have.

Let's begin!

Endnotes

i   Achor, Shawn. *The Happiness Advantage: How a Positive Brain Fuels Success in Work and Life.* New York: Currency, 2018. p.65.

ii   Stieber, Alexandra. "Tal Ben-Shahar, Positive Psychology Expert." Wunderman Thompson Intelligence, September 1, 2015. Accessed March 2, 2020. https://intelligence.wundermanthompson.com/2012/10/qa-tal-ben-shahar-positive-psychology-expert/.

iii   Robinson, Ken, and Lou Aronica. *Finding Your Element: Living a Life of Passion and Purpose.* New York: Viking, 2013. p.120.

iv   Achor, Shawn. *The Happiness Advantage: How a Positive Brain Fuels Success in Work and Life.* New York: Currency, 2018. p.40.

v   Horsley, Kevin, and Louis Fourie. *The Happy Mind: A Simple Guide to Living a Happier Life Starting Today.* Place of publication not identified: Published by TCK Publishing, 2017. p.38.

vi   Achor, Shawn. *The Happiness Advantage: How a Positive Brain Fuels Success in Work and Life.* New York: Currency, 2018. p.21.

vii   Petre, Alina. "13 Habits Linked to a Long Life (Backed by Science)." Healthline. April 8, 2019. Accessed March 2, 2020. https://www.healthline.com/nutrition/13-habits-linked-to-a-long-life.

viii   Achor, Shawn. *The Happiness Advantage: How a Positive Brain Fuels Success in Work and Life.* New York: Currency, 2018.

ix   Bstan-'dzin-rgya-mtsho and Howard C. Cutler. *The Art of Happiness: 10th Anniversary Gift Edition.* Sydney, N.S.W.: Hachette Australia, 2009.

PERCEPTIONS VISTA: SEE THE BEAUTY OF OPTIMISTIC LIVING

"Attitude is a little thing that makes a big difference."

— *Winston Churchill*

Perceptions Vista is the first stop on our journey because your outlook, or how you perceive the world, has a profound impact on your happiness. If you always look at the glass as half-empty, you will have a hard time finding joy.

Did you know that your brain receives 11 million bits of information every second from your senses? Yet it can only process 40 bits a second.[i]

Your brain has to make split-second choices about which pieces to either take in and interpret or ignore and dismiss. Therefore, **your reality is a CHOICE**. What you choose to focus on shapes your perceptions and your capability for joy.

Negativity Bias

As a successful overachiever, you have, no doubt, received many positive performance reviews, which have led to increased successes. However, you probably remember the handful of times you received negative or critical feedback much more clearly. Why is that?

This may have to do with something called **negativity bias**. Negativity bias is our tendency to notice and pay attention to negative stimuli more often than positive stimuli, and then, unfortunately, dwell on those negatives for longer. For example, you have likely forgotten all the times that you successfully traveled to and from work, but you always remember that one time when you got a flat tire or the train broke down. Because of negativity bias, you tend to:[ii]

- Remember painful experiences better than positive ones.
- Recall criticism better than praise.
- React more strongly to negative stimuli.
- Make decisions based on negative information more than positive data.

It's the "bad things" that grab our attention and stay in our memories. In studies[iii] conducted by psychologist John Cacioppo, participants were shown positive, negative, and neutral images. The researchers observed the electrical brain activity in each person and discovered that the negative images produced a much stronger electrical response than the neutral or positive images.

Additionally, studies have shown that children learn more quickly from negative feedback. In one study, during the first round, children were given an empty jar. Every time they got a right answer, they would receive one marble to put in the jar to keep. In the second round, they were given a full jar of marbles, and for every wrong answer, they would lose a marble. The study found that kids learned faster when they were losing marbles than gaining marbles, even though it was the same amount of "currency" per answer.[iv]

Negativity bias occurs not necessarily because we *want* to focus on the bad but more because we have *had* to focus on the negatives in order to survive over time. As humans evolved, in order to survive in the wild, we had to constantly be on the lookout for threats from animals and other humans. Our radars were always tuned to danger so that we could respond and react quickly.

Negativity bias is so pervasive within our beings that scientists have learned that "the amygdala uses about two-thirds of its neurons to detect negativity and then quickly stores it into long-term memory."[v]

Additionally, studies show that when we are in a negative state of mind, our brains actually perceive hills as being significantly higher and backpacks as significantly heavier. And this principle doesn't apply just to hiking. In general, when we are in a negative mindset, all loads feel heavier, all obstacles loom bigger, and all mountains seem less surmountable.[vi]

There is hope, however. Our brain has the ability to rewire itself.

Let's take a look at the underlying physiology of what happens in our brain to create negativity and positivity.

The Negative Brain vs. The Positive Brain

By no means am I a neuroscientist, but I think it's important to understand what's happening physiologically in the brain when we experience negativity as compared to positivity. **Once we understand what triggers different parts of our brain, we can engage in behaviors to favor the positive.**

- Amygdala: The amygdala is the brain's radar for threat and is constantly scanning for safety or danger. It triggers the fight-or-flight response, creates intense emotional reactions, and focuses our attention on the threat. When something worries or upsets us, the amygdala continuously brings our thoughts to that thing over and over, until it's resolved. It is the amygdala that signals the release of cortisol and adrenaline during stressful periods.

- Cortisol and adrenaline: Cortisol and adrenaline are key survival chemicals that are released during the body's stress response. Cortisol, known as the "stress hormone," increases glucose, which fuels the brain for quick decision-making and curbs functions that are non-essential in fight-or-flight situations. Adrenaline increases your heart rate, elevates your blood pressure, and boosts energy supplies so that you can fight off the threat that may be facing you.

While helpful in short-term moments of stress, prolonged states of stress can create excessively high levels of both cortisol and adrenaline which can cause:

- Anxiety
- Depression
- Irritability
- Headaches
- Weight gain
- Sleep problems
- Heart disease
- Digestive problems

- Prefrontal cortex: The functions carried out by the prefrontal cortex are known as the "executive functions." These functions include decision-making, social behavior, setting and accomplishing goals, expectation management, and personality expression. It's the part of the brain that helps you tell the difference between good and bad. It helps you to evaluate your environment and take control of your own thoughts.

When there is stronger connectivity between the prefrontal cortex and the amygdala, you are much less prone to emotional hijacking by negativity from the amygdala. The stronger the link, the less reactive you will be.

- Dopamine, serotonin, and endorphins:
  ◊ Dopamine is the central chemical that regulates how you experience pleasure and reward. During pleasurable moments or situations, this neurotransmitter is released, causing you to seek out a desirable activity repeatedly. Additionally, dopamine receptors in the prefrontal cortex enhance working memory. For example, you will remember an enjoyable experience, such as a very tasty meal, more vividly and for a longer time period than an average meal.

  ◊ Serotonin is your natural mood stabilizer. When levels of serotonin are normal, you feel happier, calmer, more focused, less anxious, and emotionally more stable. If serotonin is out of balance or lacking, you may feel sad for no reason, worried, or overwhelmed. You may lose interest in your favorite activities, foods, friendships, and relationships.

  ◊ Endorphins are natural pain relievers and pleasure boosters. Endorphins are released when you are injured, experience stress, or activate your natural reward system with activities like eating or exercising. I envision endorphins to be like little Pac-Men who eat cortisol and adrenaline for lunch when you are trying to improve your mood or decrease anxiety.

Understanding what happens in your brain and body can help you overcome negativity bias and negative emotions in order to better pursue joy. Since your thoughts create a cascade of chemical releases, you truly do have some control over your emotional well-being.

For overachievers, it's important to understand how stress negatively impacts our brains. In one study, brain scans of people who worked up to 70 hours a week for a year showed enlarged amygdalae and weak connections between areas in the prefrontal cortex.[vii] That means that the amygdala has been running wild with little control, creating fear, anxiety, and a constant rush of adrenaline and cortisol.

But there is good news, and that good news is called neuroplasticity.

Neuroplasticity is the brain's amazing capacity to change, adapt, and essentially "rewire" itself. By working to focus on the positive, such as engaging the prefrontal cortex to maintain appropriate levels of dopamine, serotonin, and endorphins, it is possible to overcome negativity bias.

Imagine if the larger percentage of the 40 bits of information that your brain can process in a second was on the positive side. What if you actively tried to look for the good in a situation or person? **Much like any other muscle, you can train your brain towards joy.**

Wouldn't it be fantastic if you could create an optimism bias?

The Power of Optimism

With optimism and positivity, your body is awash with dopamine, serotonin, and endorphins, and your prefrontal cortex has a good handle over your amygdala. Think about it. When you're feeling happy, you carry yourself differently. You have a spring in your step, smile easily, interact with others in a friendly way, have more patience, and are more open to new experiences. With positivity, you are literally immersed in a different biochemical wash.

Optimism and positivity create a long list of benefits in the body:

- Lower blood pressure
- Fewer colds
- Better sleep
- Achievement of more goals

- Less pain
- Lower disease risks
- Better stress management
- Ability to overcome obstacles more easily

This isn't to say that you don't encounter any negative experiences, situations, or emotions. You will. It's more about *how you handle those moments so as to lean towards positivity.* Honor and embrace your sadness, fear, anger, or disappointment. Acknowledge your feelings and let them pass through. They won't last long if you allow yourself to feel them fully, to discharge the energy they hold. Once you release this energy, you can move back towards the positive side.

Just like we trained our brains over human evolution to pick up on threats and dangers, we can also train our brains for positivity. We need to actively become more attuned to noticing and savoring joy, happiness, and gratitude. Science claims that *we can implant a positive experience into our long-term memory by paying attention to it for only 10–20 seconds.*[viii] So it doesn't take much effort to start to turn the tide.

How do you begin? There is a variety of ways you can start to re-train your brain towards a positivity bias.

Gratitude

Expressing gratitude is one of the easiest ways to shift our perceptions from the negative towards the positive. Not surprisingly, numerous studies attest to its benefits. Grateful people:

- Are 25% more happy than others.
- Are more energetic.

- Are more emotionally intelligent.
- Are more forgiving.

- Are less likely to be depressed, anxious, or lonely.
- Feel more socially connected.
- Enjoy better quality sleep.
- Have better dietary habits.

Here are some ways[ix] to engage in gratitude on a frequent basis:

1. Keep a gratitude journal and add to it several times a week.
2. Tell someone you love them and how much you appreciate them.
3. Notice the beauty in nature each day.
4. Smile more often.
5. Watch inspiring videos that remind you of the good in the world.
6. Include an act of kindness in your life each day.
7. Volunteer for organizations that help others.
8. Spend quality time with your family.
9. Give a compliment daily.
10. Send a physical card in your own handwriting.
11. Give recognition to a colleague.
12. Say thank you for the little things around the house, things you would normally take for granted.
13. If someone does something nice for you, do something nice for them.
14. Meditate with your gratitude list, giving thanks for all your good fortune.
15. Thank the people who serve you in the community—the shopkeepers, the bus drivers, etc.
16. Send love to your enemies or people you dislike.
17. Be thankful when you learn something new.
18. See the growth opportunity in your mistakes.
19. Share gratitude with your family during mealtimes.
20. Appreciate yourself.

I find gratitude incredibly powerful. It helps me to shift my attention away from myself to those around me, to notice and acknowledge them. In many cases, the thoughts are occurring in my head anyway, such as appreciation for my husband doing the dishes or the great point made by a client during a meeting; showing gratitude is a matter of being sure to express it out loud. Additionally, the receiver, typically, lights up when they are acknowledged, which makes me feel good.

If expressing gratitude isn't something you do regularly, select a day or even a week to make it your focus. Be as generous as possible with your gratitude and see how it works for your positivity.

Meditation/Mindfulness

Meditation has been around for thousands of years, and its practice is like taking your brain to the gym. Its use has seen a dramatic increase in the US over the last decade. According to an NIH and CDC study in 2017, the number of Americans who practiced meditation tripled between 2012 and 2017.[x] Meditation is a useful stress- and negativity-reduction technique because it increases the connection to the prefrontal cortex to keep the amygdala under control, as well as lowering cortisol levels.

Mindfulness, a type of meditation that focuses on the "now," has its origins in the US with Jon Kabat-Zinn. A student of Zen Buddhism teachings since 1965, he founded the Stress Reduction Clinic at the University of Massachusetts Medical School in 1979. He adapted Buddhist teachings on mindfulness and developed the Stress Reduction and Relaxation program, which he later renamed the "Mindfulness-Based Stress Reduction" (MBSR) program.[xi] There have since been over 600 published studies[xii] on MBSR and its benefits. For example:

- Volunteers, who had never meditated before, engaged in mindfulness and meditated for 20 minutes a day for one week. Then they had a brain scan. During the scan, they were shown images ranging from gruesome burn victims to cute bunnies. They watched these images in their everyday state of mind and then while practicing mindfulness. During mindfulness, their amygdala response to all the images was significantly lower (compared to non-meditators).

- In another study, the amygdala showed dampened activity from a mere 30 or so hours of MBSR practice. And over time, with more practice, the reactivity of the amygdala continued to lessen. Practitioners became more immune to emotional hijacking because their brains had a stronger connectivity between the prefrontal cortex and the amygdala.

- Those who had taken Kabat-Zinn's course were shown to experience less stress, less pain, reduced anxiety, clearer skin, and better immune functioning.

- A study from UCLA found that meditation slowed the brain from shrinking as we age. At age 50, meditators' brains were 7.5 years "younger" than brains of nonmeditators of the same age.

Overall, with high levels of mindfulness practice, emotions seem to lose their power to pull us into their melodrama.

So what exactly is mindfulness and how do you practice it? Kabat-Zinn describes mindfulness as "a means of paying attention in a particular way—on purpose, in the present moment, and nonjudgmentally."[xiii] The goal is to note the thought, emotion, or sensory impression and then to let it go. Avoid dwelling on it. Let it flow in and then flow out without reaction. You learn to accept a thought as just a thought and choose not to magnify it. With a negative thought, if you are able to let it go, then you've disarmed it.

Meditation, generally, and mindfulness, specifically, is best practiced with help from others. There are so many sources available, from books to classes to apps, so I encourage you to do some research and then simply try it. You will need to explore to see if you prefer guided meditation or just sound; if an app will work for you or if you prefer to be with others in a class; if you want to explore the history of meditation to understand how it will work for you before you try it.

Try not to get discouraged if you don't "feel" anything at the outset. Meditation has been around for thousands of years because it takes *practice.*

I am still on the learning curve for meditation, having only started practicing within the last year. I like using the Calm app, and when I can really clear my mind, I feel great afterwards. My biggest challenge is fitting it into my day. I like to meditate first thing in the morning, before my brain gets too busy, but it hasn't yet become a habit. I sometimes forget to make the time as mornings are also my time to exercise, which is a habit, a hobby, and a necessary staple in my life.

Exercise

Most people think about the body's benefits from exercise, but **exercise is also excellent for the brain and for positivity.**

Specifically, aerobic exercise that produces a sweat and gets your blood pumping is the best. With aerobic exercise, dopamine, serotonin, and endorphins are released. In addition, norepinephrine and BDNF are discharged. Norepinephrine helps you to become more alert and focused, as well as boosts memory retrieval. BDNF (brain-derived neurotrophic factor) helps to create new connections between nerve cells and repairs cells that are damaged. It's a direct contributor to neuroplasticity, and exercise increases brain production of BDNF by up to three times.[xiv]

How much exercise is needed to release these chemicals and see benefits? The 2018 Physical Activity Guidelines[xv] suggest:

- 150 minutes of moderate aerobic activity a week
- Any activity is better than no activity
- Exercise needs to be regular and consistent for the best results

Manage the Negativity Spinout

Anxiety and worry can stir up an enormous amount of negativity if left unchecked. There are two situations in particular where these feelings can spin out of control: a distressing event and an uncontrollable situation. Both are manageable, and the key is to not let the amygdala run amuck and leave you in a constant state of worry and despair. Here are some techniques that can help.

A Distressing Event

As a public speaker, it can be tough to please everyone in the room. Everyone is a critic. Early on in my career of delivering training programs, I would regularly wake up in the middle of the night sweating, in a panic. Did yesterday's participants like the workshop? Did that joke rub someone the wrong way? In telling a story, did I violate a confidence? Would I be hired again? I lost hours of sleep from worry.

After a while, I knew I had to take control of this anxiety or I would never survive my chosen profession. I asked myself the following questions:

- How often has this negative event happened to me in the past?
- Is this negative event unique to me or does it happen to others as well?
- Is it a situation that others have managed to a reasonable outcome?
- What are all the potential outcomes (good or bad)?
- What is the percentage likelihood for each of those outcomes?
- What is the absolute worst outcome that could happen? What is its percentage likelihood of happening?

- Is there anything I can do to influence the situation towards a positive outcome?
- Can I live with the high percentage of bad outcomes? If any of them do happen, what would be my response?

I realized that the outcomes that I feared—participants not liking the program, offending someone, and not getting hired again—weren't happening. In fact, the opposite was happening. Responses to the workshops were positive, and my business was flourishing.

So when you find yourself in the throes of a perceived distressing event, ask yourself these questions to help you find the reality of the situation or to get yourself into a more rational state of mind. Your responses to these questions will hopefully control the spin-out and focus you on what's most important for the situation.

Control the Controllables

There are many variations of quotes out there about controlling what you can control and letting go of the rest. Yet we can still fall prey to the worry and anxiety about the uncontrollables. Air travel used to be a big worry for me until I finally put it under my "control lens."

When I started traveling a lot for my business, I would fret, almost uncontrollably, about late airplanes and missed flights due to weather or other airline delays. I worried that I wouldn't arrive in time to deliver the training programs that my clients were paying me for. I figured out quickly that this reaction was not sustainable, especially because I was regularly on at least five airplanes a week.

To get a handle on my anxiety, I broke down all the steps of my travel to evaluate what I could control. Then I assessed the potential outcomes of those aspects that I could not control.

Can Control	Can't Control
1. Getting to the airport	1. Traffic to the airport
2. Getting to my gate	2. The security line
3. Time between connecting flights	3. A timely arrival of the inbound plane for my flight
4. Getting to my connecting flight	4. The weather
5. Allowing for delays in order to still make it to the client on time	5. A timely arrival of the crew
	6. A timely departure of my flight
	7. A timely arrival of my flight
	8. For connecting flights, repeat #3–#7

Once I did this analysis, I realized that there are up to three times the number of factors that are completely out of my control. My worry was completely unproductive for those factors. My most important concern was #5 on the "Can Control" list—making it to the client on time. After this analysis, I decided to always travel the night before a client engagement. I knew I would worry way too much if I tried to travel on the morning of the important meeting.

If you have regularly occurring activities in your life that are causing you a fair amount of consternation, such as your commute, interactions with certain co-workers or getting dinner on the table—ask yourself the distressing event questions or put it under your own control lens.

In essence: put the prefrontal cortex to work in order to manage the amygdala response and strive to limit the negativity or emotional reaction to only what is appropriate or necessary.

Kindness

Most of us think that acts of kindness are good for the receiver, but multitudes of studies show that it is incredibly impactful for the giver, as well.

Acts of kindness only need seconds to occur.

According to Dartmouth College,[xvi] kindness releases serotonin and oxytocin. Oxytocin, known as the "love hormone," helps to lower blood pressure, increase self-esteem and optimism, and improve heart health. Research from Emory University reveals that your brain's pleasure and reward centers light up as if you were the recipient of the kindness, not the giver. This is commonly referred to as the "helper's high." Perpetually kind people have 23% less cortisol and age more slowly than the average population in the US.

A University of British Columbia study showed that a group of highly anxious individuals, who performed at least six acts of kindness a week for one month, experienced a significant increase in positive moods and relationship satisfaction and a decrease in social avoidance.

So get out there and be kind. There are numerous websites and sources of ideas to spur your kindness. Here a few to begin your journey:

- Say hello or smile at strangers
- Write a note to someone who isn't expecting it
- Buy the coffee of the person behind you
- Write letters to soldiers
- Babysit for free
- Take the time to listen to someone
- Volunteer your time
- Give up your place in line to another person
- Make breakfast in bed for your partner
- Hold the door open for someone
- Walk the neighbor's dog
- Run a 5K for a good cause

Affirmations

Affirmations are positive statements that encourage an optimistic mindset, motivate you, inspire positive changes, or boost self-esteem.

I admit that I was skeptical about the use of affirmations at first, but I have found they can be helpful. They focus me on areas where I want to think and behave differently for the better.

The purpose of an affirmation is not to change anything outside of yourself but to change the way you feel about a specific area of your life. When you feel differently about something, you will start to think and believe differently about it. And when you feel, think, and believe differently, you will take alternate actions and other, more positive experiences will manifest in your life.

For example, my perception of my body has been a lifelong struggle for me. I have often avoided full-length mirrors in the bathroom because I don't like what I see. I am incredibly critical of my flaws and often wish my body was smaller, sexier, and more attractive.

However, avoiding full-length mirrors doesn't fix my problem. I need to learn how to see the beauty rather than the flaws when I look in the mirror. I want to feel as confident about my body as I do about the rest of me. So I have been working with a mantra of "My body is a projection of the confidence that I have in myself." It has enabled me, little by little, to see the positivity radiating from within me, rather than all of my perceived "flaws." I feel better about my body, which helps me to believe that I am sexy and attractive, which, by the way, is what my husband has always believed.

The key to affirmations is repetition. You could recite your affirmations once each morning, once each evening, both morning and evening, or even more frequently during the day. It only needs to take a few minutes. You repeat them until they become a regular part of your thinking process, leading to a consistent way of behaving. ThinkUp and Shine are two examples of apps that can help you determine your affirmations, which you should then keep them in front of you throughout your day.

You now have six methods to help you overcome negativity bias and move towards positivity and optimism. Try one. Try all six. Find what works for you and reap the benefits of joyful perceptions.

Endnotes

i   Achor, Shawn. *Before Happiness: The 5 Hidden Keys to Achieving Success, Spreading Happiness, and Sustaining Positive Change.* New York: Crown Business, 2013.

ii   Cherry, Kendra. "What is the Negativity Bias?" Verywell Mind. April 29, 2020. Accessed April 29, 2020.https://www.verywellmind.com/negative-bias-4589618.

iii Berkovic, Eva. "Why Does Your Brain Love Negativity? The Negativity Bias." Marbella International University Centre, February 09, 2017. Accessed April 22, 2020. https://www.miuc.org/brain-love-negativity-negativity-bias/.

iv   Suttie, Jill. "How to Overcome Your Brain's Fixation on Bad Things." *Greater Good Magazine.* Accessed April 22, 2020. https://greatergood.berkeley.edu/article/item/how_to_overcome_your_brains_fixation_on_bad_things.

v   Berkovic, Eva. "Why Does Your Brain Love? Negativity? The Negativity Bias." Marbella International University Centre, February 09, 2017. Accessed April 22, 2020. https://www.miuc.org/brain-love-negativity-negativity-bias/.

vi   Achor, Shawn. *The Happiness Advantage: How a Positive Brain Fuels Success in Work and Life.* New York: Currency, 2018. p.15

vii Golkar, Armita, Emilia Johansson, Maki Kasahara, Walter Osika, Aleksander Perski and Ivanka Savic. "The Influence of Work-Related Chronic Stress on the Regulation of Emotion and on Functional Connectivity in the Brain." (2014) *PLoS ONE* 9(9). https://journals.plos.org/plosone/article?id=10.1371/journal.pone.0104550.

viii Hanson, Rick. *Hardwiring Happiness: The New Brain Science of Contentment, Calm, and Confidence.* New York: Harmony Books, 2016.

ix   Conlon, Ciara. "40 Simple Ways To Practice Gratitude." Lifehack. July 08, 2019. Accessed April 19, 2020.https://www.lifehack.org/articles/communication/40-simple-ways-practice-gratitude.html.

x   Dockrill, Peter. "There's a Strange Explosion of Certain Meditative Practices in America Right Now." ScienceAlert. November 12, 2018. Accessed July 03, 2020. https://www.sciencealert.com/yoga-and-meditation-in-the-us-are-totally-exploding-right-now.

xi   Shea, Christopher. "A Brief History of Mindfulness in the USA and Its Impact on Our Lives." Psych Central. October 08, 2018. Accessed April 22, 2020. https://psychcentral.com/lib/a-brief-history-of-mindfulness-in-the-usa-and-its-impact-on-our-lives/.

xii Goleman, Daniel, and Richard J. Davidson. *Altered Traits: Science Reveals How Meditation Changes Your Mind, Brain, and Body.* New York, NY: Avery, an imprint of Penguin Random House LLC, 2018.

xiii Shea, Christopher. "A Brief History of Mindfulness in the USA and Its Impact on Our Lives." Psych Central, October 8, 2018. Accessed April 22, 2020.https://psychcentral.com/lib/a-brief-history-of-mindfulness-in-the-usa-and-its-impact-on-our-lives/.

xiv Friedrich, Cathe. "5 Brain-Boosting Chemicals Released During Exercise."

Cathe. March 24, 2019. Accessed April 22, 2020. https://cathe.com/5-brain-boosting-chemicals-released-during-exercise/.

xv   HHS Office and President's Council on Sports, Fitness, and Nutrition. "Physical Activity Guidelines for Americans." HHS.gov. February 01, 2019. Accessed April 22, 2020.   https://www.hhs.gov/fitness/be-active/physical-activity-guidelines-for-americans/index.html.

xvi   Dartmouth College. "Kindness Health Facts." Accessed 06 August, 2020. https://www.dartmouth.edu/wellness/emotional/rakhealthfacts.pdf.

VALUES VILLAGE: DISCOVER WHAT REALLY MAKES YOU TICK

"It's not hard to make decisions when you know
what your values are."

— *Roy Disney*

Values awaken the "why" in your life.

Values are the beliefs that motivate or drive you to behave in one way or another. Put another way, values are the undercurrent by which you make decisions and define your priorities. They help you to decide whom to marry, whom to work for, where to spend your money, how to spend your time, etc. They are a foundation for joy and a cornerstone of your True Self and who you are meant to be.

Most people do not have enough clarity about their values. If I ask someone if they know their priority values, they might pause, look off into space to think and then say, "Sure, I know my values. I think it would be my family. Yes, family is my most important value."

When I hear this type of response, I have a few thoughts:

1. Family is only one value, and I believe that there is more than one value that a person lives by.
2. Are you saying family because you feel that's the answer you *should* give?
3. Because you had to think about it and only came up with one value, it's clear to me that you haven't spent time getting clear about all of the values that drive your life.

This is not a judgment, merely an observation.

Values Clarity

Many, if not most, people don't have clarity about their values.

- They don't take the time to do the necessary self-exploration or haven't given much thought to their values.
- They are exposed to a values exercise but blow it off or put the paper aside, never to be read again.
- They think that values don't really matter.

Whatever the reason, people live a rudderless life when they are not clear about their values.

The biggest consequence of not knowing your values is that you could live an unhappy or unfulfilled life that isn't attached to anything. **It is a life without meaning.** It is a life that doesn't propel you toward who you are meant to be. It is a life of decisions that aren't rooted in your True Self.

Values for Joychievers

Take an overachiever. As an overachiever you live your life in reaction to others' values and choices. You let these values guide your decision-making—where to attend university, what profession to pursue, which partner to choose, etc. After making all those decisions, however, you realize that you are unhappy. You haven't taken the opportunity to uncover your own values to discover your True Self and what makes YOU most happy.

Everyone has their own unique set of values. There are no right or wrong values. It's important to identify the values that are meaningful for YOU.

I didn't have clarity about my top values until my early 30's, and when I achieved it, suddenly so many of the reasons for my life choices and decisions became abundantly obvious. I quickly realized which decisions I'd made throughout my life had aligned with my values and which hadn't.

- Why one job felt like a dream and another hadn't.
- Why a particular love partner was a mismatch.
- Why one friend became a best friend.
- Why I avoided certain hobbies.
- Why some volunteer moments lit up my soul.

It truly was an awakening—like a veil had been lifted on all the choices I had made to that point. I vowed, from then on, to always consult my values when making life decisions.

It is critical to know your values well enough that you can quickly list them at any time. For example, my current values are joy, excellence, curiosity, purpose, self-discipline, and variety. I say current because values can change over time. In the process that led up to writing this book, I had some self-exploration moments that caused me to deprioritize one value and add another.

I would expect the same for you. **As your life circumstances change, your values may change.** If you have a child, your values may change. If you become single, your values may change. If you learn and develop more of your strengths, your values may change. If you lose a loved one, your values may change. Your values don't change every day, but momentous times in your life may create an adjustment.

Let me describe how my personal values have played out in my life.

Joy, for me, is about meaningful fun. I want to have meaningful fun as often as I can and in as many aspects of my life as possible. This does not mean that I can't be serious, that I am frivolous, or that I have to pack fun into every moment. But I do look for work, activities and people that make me smile easily, warm my insides, and fill my joy bucket.

Excellence has been a lifelong value. Since I was a kid, I have paid a high level of attention to performing at the highest level possible for me. I strive to be excellent in my work and create experiences that clients find extremely valuable. This excellence value has paid off over time with accolades, great reviews, and loyal, long-term clients.

Curiosity prevents me from getting bored. I love to learn, and I get a thrill from creating new things. Every job I have ever had has been a new role for the company I joined. In all my work, I have created things—a new curriculum, new workshops, new lines of business, this book, etc. Curiosity was critical in selecting a life partner too. I wanted to be with someone who, like me, wanted to explore the world and have new experiences. This resulted in my husband and I visiting 11 countries in one year.

Purpose, for me, is about living a life in a goal-oriented or driven way. I have always been thoughtful around setting goals for myself and then working to accomplish them. I like to have something to aim at, whether that be in my personal life or in my professional life. I need to have a destination. It happens to give me a lot of joy.

Self-discipline manifests itself in several ways for me. It helps me to stay focused on my goals. It helps me to avoid eating too many cookies in one sitting. It helps me to stay consistent with exercising four to five times a week. It helps me to feel in control of my life and stay true to the course of continuously seeking joy, as I define it.

These happen to be my values, and I encourage you to seek clarity about yours. For those of you who think that values are fluffy or mushy or ask why you should bother to identify them, take note:

You are living by them anyhow.

Whether you realize it or not, the choices you make are based on something. Not identifying your values leads you to simply overachieving, rather than joychieving.

At a minimum, you will feel unfulfilled at some point. If you keep wondering why things aren't working out or think you should feel happier, it may be because you haven't identified your priority values. Values add robustness to a person's life.

Let me tell you about my friend, Sarah. Sarah is a successful business owner and entrepreneur. She volunteers at her church, is active in her community, and is a proud mother of three. She is in constant action.

During one of our conversations, she revealed that she was not happy in her work life. Sarah shared that she has super high expectations of herself. She often sets goals that are unattainable, which sets her up to always feel like a failure.

When she does accomplish a goal, Sarah either, 1) focuses immediately on the next goal without celebrating the accomplishment or 2) goes into self-critical mode to consider how she could have performed better. And, sometimes, she does both.

She suffers from a lot of anxiety and guilt about never being good enough.

Sarah wonders if she can ever break this pattern to simply feel happy or content. In fact, she once said, "Being me and 'joy' are diametrically opposed. I *cannot* do both. The overachieving need is so strong, it always seems to take over."

I asked Sarah if she had ever spent time examining her values. Like many, she said she once had to do it for a "work thing" but didn't remember what they were. So she agreed to do my Values Sort Exercise (see below). Through this exercise, she discovered that her top values and associated definitions were:

- Accomplishment: Setting goals, reaching achievement, not doing things halfway.
- Excellence: Doing things "right" the first time.
- Mercy: Expressing forgiveness and compassion, especially when someone may not necessarily deserve it.
- Responsibility: wning up to what is yours (good or bad) and not avoiding difficult conversations when needed.

Seeing these values on paper were an epiphany for her. They didn't instantly solve her happiness dilemma, but they helped to explain some of what she was feeling.

While she loved the satisfaction of accomplishing her goals, the dark side of that value is that she didn't allow herself to enjoy the moment. I offered that she might want to consider setting smaller, more incremental goals so that the big goals didn't weigh so heavily on her mind. Additionally, by setting shorter, more achievable goals, she would have more opportunities to practice a different reaction when she attained them.

Sarah invested heavily—research, learning, time—in always trying to do things right the first time. Was that level of investment always necessary? Did *everything* have to be right the *first* time? Can an iterative process be helpful? How could she rely more on others to help?

While she expressed mercy for others regularly, she was stingy when it came to how she viewed herself. In some cases, she was the one who needed compassion the most and needed to learn how to give *herself* a break more often.

Being responsible came easily to her. While not always pleasant, Sarah wasn't afraid to have tough conversations when needed and took pride in that ability.

Going through this exercise gave Sarah more insights into what made her, *her*. She could work on ways to leverage her values to her advantage, as well as how to manage their relationship to her overachiever ways.

Six months after she had gained clarity on her values, I revisited Sarah. During that time, the economic market had wreaked havoc with her businesses, and at one point, she thought she was going to lose everything. It had been tough for her. At the time of our conversation, though, she had secured some financial help and was feeling much more hopeful about the future of her businesses.

When I asked her how she had utilized her values during that time, Sarah reflected that she felt positive about how her values had helped to guide her actions. She had spent a lot of time researching, reading, and talking with others to find the right way to help her businesses, and it was looking like that effort would pay off. For example, her responsibility value had pushed her to find creative ways to help her financial position so she could retain all of her team.

Sarah let herself feel the unhappiness and despair of her situation. She accepted that it wasn't a sign that she was a failure, and she didn't have to automatically move into action to resolve those negative feelings. She could simply feel them, process them, and then let them go.

Sarah let her values help guide her though this challenging period and enable her to make some great decisions. While she may not have been at a place of complete joy, having clarified her values, she felt much more grounded and positive about how she had managed that time in her business.

Values Sort Exercise

So how do you figure out your values? On www.joychiever.com and in the appendix of this book, you will find an extensive (though not exhaustive) list of values and their corresponding general definitions.

Your goal is to get to your top five to ten priority values.

1. From my website, print the Values list and cut them into "cards."

2. Go through the cards and create three piles: Yes, No, and Maybe.

- "Yes" are values that most resonate with you and are a priority.
- "No" values don't necessarily speak to you.
- "Maybe" means it could be a priority value, but you are not sure yet.

If there are other words or values that you feel should be included in the starter list, please feel free to add them.

There are a couple of thoughts to keep in mind as you go through the list.

Putting a value in the "No" pile doesn't mean that it's a bad value or that you are a bad person for not including it in your priority "Yes" list. For example, compassion is in my "No" pile. This doesn't mean that I don't have concern for others and their challenges. It just doesn't rise to my top five to ten values.

Your "Yes" pile values should reflect the real you, not the ideal of how you want to or should behave. I wish I could incorporate more philanthropy into my life, but my work schedule and business make that more challenging. Supporting and giving to my community are important, but I make other choices for how to spend my time, such as taking a trip to a new destination, over philanthropy.

When you have gone through the values list once, you should have your three piles.

3. Tackle your "Maybe" list and try to separate them into "Yes" or "No."

If you struggle with this step, think back to important moments in your life and reflect on the types of decisions that you made or actions that you took. Consider why you ended a relationship or selected one job over another. Think about how you spend your free time and why. Contemplate a tumultuous time in your life and how you found your way through it. See if these reflections on the way you acted in your past can give you clues about your values and help sort your "Maybe" list.

4. Focus on your "Yes" list.

I want you to try to get your "Yes" pile down to 20–25 values. Then lay out all the values in front of you and see if there are any emerging themes. I had "adventure," "challenge," "curiosity," and "learning" in my pile. To me, they are all related, so I chose "curiosity" as the main representative value for the four.

Continue to look for themes and whittle down your pile until you have five to ten values.

The next step in this process is a critical one.

5. You need to write your own definition for each of your values.

The same value can mean different things to different people, so it's important that you are clear about what it means for you. For example, the dictionary definition of joy is "intense and especially ecstatic or exultant happiness." My personal definition of joy isn't quite so intense. I consider joy to be more about fun or enjoyment and having moments that bring a smile to my face.

Now that you have your priority values and have written down what they mean to you, you can use them as guides for future decision-making. Keep them handy. Consult them often.

Utilize them as your own personal oracle.

STRENGTHS MOUNTAIN: MAKE THE BEST PART OF YOUR JOB THE BIGGEST PART OF YOUR JOB

"If you spend your life trying to be good at everything, you will never be great at anything."

— *Tom Rath*

Everyone is good at something. **Each time we use a skill, whatever it is, we experience a burst of positivity.** Yet only 17% of us have our strengths in play most of the time.[i] Additionally, when asked how often we feel an emotional high at work—a sign that we're playing to a strength—51% of us say "about once a week."[ii]

There are three possible reasons for those numbers being too low:

1. You haven't spent enough time working to identify your true strengths and the specific environments in which your strengths could excel.
2. You have been listening to too many other people about what your strengths should be and what career you should pursue.

3. You have some strong skills and have pursued jobs comprised of those skills. Yet they're not true strengths because they don't invigorate, inspire, or provide joy regularly.

Many of these applied to Brandy, a successful real estate agent. She was the child of parents who both worked as teachers, so going to college was a sure thing for her. Brandy had always wanted to help people, so she pursued a degree in social work. Real estate wasn't even on her radar at the time.

Upon graduating, she got a job in a law office as an administrative professional. It was a safe job that gave her a paycheck. After a few years, she did eventually move into social work. She took a job at a senior living facility that incorporated both social work and property management. She enjoyed helping the residents who needed support and coordination for their care and services.

During that time, she had begun to think that real estate, rather than social work and property management, might be an interesting career path so she committed to getting her license. However, she only completed one transaction. Personal things in Brandy's life kept her from moving into real estate, and it took her another 12 years to realize that real estate was her true passion and to finally make that leap.

During those 12 years, she worked to develop her natural talents in other areas:

- Being able to connect with people
- Providing a calming influence during tough moments and drama
- Demonstrating authenticity, honesty, and patience
- Organizing processes and working with numbers

This is a great combination of strengths for a real estate professional to have. It took some time for Brandy to gather the courage to move into the profession—to make the choice for her joy—but now that she has, her heart sings. Brandy can't imagine doing anything else, and she leverages her True Self strengths daily.

Joychievers need to strive to use their strengths, in some capacity, on a daily basis.

As overachievers, we have an instinct for what we are good at, but there is so much more to explore. We spend one-third of our lives working. If playing to a strength once a week is the best we can do, then this is a problem. On top of that, 49% of us are not using our strengths even once a week. This is a significant area of missed opportunity for joy.

Utilizing your strengths in everyday life has been linked to:[iii]

- An elevated sense of vitality and motivation
- An increased probability of achieving goals
- A stronger sense of life direction
- Higher self-confidence, engagement, and productivity

The goal is to find your True Self strengths. Take out a blank piece of paper. You will be making notes and lists as you walk through the seven steps below to identify and clarify the specific strengths that bring you the most joy.

Step One: Think About What Talents Come Naturally

You are born with a specific set of natural talents. Some of these talents may have shown themselves in childhood, and others may still be hidden because the opportunity to use them hasn't yet arisen. Natural talents can lead to strengths. If you work with your inborn gifts, these skills may come more easily and be more fun to use than other skills that you might develop through schooling, training, or experience.

Once you find opportunities to use your natural talents and discover that you enjoy using them, you need to develop them until they become a strength. It may take much less effort to become good at something that comes naturally to you than at something that doesn't, but if you don't make that effort, you won't grow that talent into a strength.

Take John Legend, for example. He is a musical marvel. He is one of only 15 people to have received EGOT status—by winning an Emmy, a Grammy, an Oscar, and a Tony. People called him a child prodigy when he started playing the piano at three and singing solos with his church choir at six. He clearly is naturally gifted. However, this gift doesn't automatically make him into an award-winning musician. He still practiced for countless hours and spent the beginning of his career as a session musician while he honed his craft.

To come up with a list of your natural talents, consider the following questions:

- What sorts of activities or skills come easily to you?
- How did you first become aware of them?
- How have you spent time developing those skills?
- Do you have any talents that you haven't developed but wish that you had?
- Do you have any talents that you have been discouraged from developing?
- Which of your talents do you think you could really develop if you tried?

Start a list of the *talents* that appear in your answers to these questions.

Step Two: Ask Others About Your Strengths

People who know you observe your strengths regularly, even daily.

At work, you receive performance feedback from your boss. Your peers ask you to join their teams to leverage your strengths for a particular task. Your family and friends witness your strengths grow over time. It's important to tap into these sources to understand what others consider to be your strengths.

Consider your performance reviews over the years. For which skills do you regularly receive exemplary praise? Look especially for those skills that rise to the top. Ask your family and friends what they think you are best at. Talk with the people with whom you share hobbies, interests, volunteer time, or other activities. When they think of you, what skills first come to mind? If they needed something done, in which situations would they call you?

For this step, add *strengths* to your talents from Step One.

Step Three: Reflect on Your Crowning Moments

There are various ways to think about "crowning moments." While using a skill or strength, you:

- Feel that the task is easy, almost effortless.
- Feel like you were in your groove.
- Become immersed and lose yourself in the activity.
- Stay naturally focused and feel like time flies by.
- Accomplish a great goal or achievement.

Take a walk down memory lane and think about the jobs that you have had. Did you have any crowning moments? For each moment, write down the scenario, the activities in which you engaged, and the corresponding skills that you used. Which of those skills fit the descriptions from the list above?

For this step, add *skills* to your talents and strengths list.

Step Four: Capture Your Specific Strengths

By now you will have a few lists on the go: talents, strengths, and skills. The next step is to identify which of those talents, strengths, and skills are your *most joyous strengths*, those activities in which you demonstrate consistent, near-perfect performance while simultaneously experiencing joy.

These are the strengths that energize you, seem effortless, and challenge you in a productive way. You may say things like, "This is fun!" or "I could do this forever," about these strengths. You want to engage them regularly and retain an appetite for more. Highlight the strengths on your list that fall into that category.

One word of caution—you will undoubtably be good at things you don't enjoy. They may bore you and drain you. You can do them and do them well, but if you never had to do them again, you wouldn't miss them. While these activities are indeed strengths, they are not the strengths that you want to focus on as a Joychiever.

You want to stay focused on your most joyous strengths. For example, administrative tasks, such as logistics, meeting planning, paperwork, filing, organization, and billing, are not a strength for me. I can do them (and have to do them because I am a company of one), but they are NOT fun or enjoyable. I regularly consider hiring a virtual assistant.

While steps one to three started you on a good list of your strengths, it's important to ensure that you don't miss out any strengths because they didn't occur to you in your analysis, you haven't yet developed them, or aren't in a job that leverages them.

In order to identify these "dormant strengths," let's continue your analysis by examining "hard" skills and "soft" skills relevant to you.

- "Hard" skills are the technical skills of your chosen profession. There are observable and measurable and are often improved with training. Hard skills can include "drafting" for architects or "suturing a wound" for doctors, for example.
- "Soft" skills reflect personal or interpersonal behavior. They typically fall into the categories of communication, critical thinking, relationship-building, leadership, and teaming.

Think about all the jobs you have had and be sure to include any and all hard skills that may have brought you joy. Additionally, listed below are examples of soft skills. Review and add any that may be missing from your list.

Adaptability	Business ethics	Business etiquette
Collaboration	Conflict resolution	Critical thinking
Decision-making	Delegation	Dispute resolution
Emotional intelligence	Empathy	Facilitation
Giving feedback	Innovation	Intercultural competence
Interpersonal relationships	Listening	Managing difficult conversations
Negotiation	Organization	Persuasion
Planning	Problem-solving	Public speaking
Receiving criticism	Resilience	Self-confidence
Strategic planning	Stress management	Supervising
Team-building	Time management	Tolerance of change and uncertainty
Verbal Communication	Visual communication	Writing

Now that you have a list of your most joyous strengths, there is one more level of analysis you need to do to get to your True Self strengths.

Step Five: Explore Best-Fit Contexts

It's not enough to create your list of strengths and stop there. To get to the highest levels of joy you also have to consider the contexts in which you utilize those strengths. Context can have a significant impact on joy.

Public speaking is a natural talent for me. I have stood out from peers in giving presentations since I was 12 years old. It has always been a skill that brings me satisfaction. I really enjoy seeing audience members learn something new and dig into how they can assimilate these new concepts into their daily work.

After starting my new business, where I was delivering at least three presentations a week, I found myself feeling bored. I wasn't very joyful, and I couldn't understand it. I was in control of my own destiny, doing what I loved, and having success. Why was I bored?

Upon reflection, I realized that there were some contexts in particular that I enjoyed much more than others. It wasn't enough to be able to use my public-speaking strength regularly. I was most invigorated when I was in front of an audience who:

- Was highly interested in using what I was teaching them;
- Engaged with me during the session;
- Shared their own challenges and looked to me for help;
- Challenged what I was teaching as they tried to assimilate the concepts into their jobs; or
- Found immediate benefit from using the concepts I was teaching.

When audiences didn't engage in this way, public speaking wasn't as enjoyable for me. So in order for you to reach the highest level of joy, not only do you need to look at your strengths but also the contexts you use them in that you enjoy most.

Strengths + Contexts = Joy

What are those contexts for you? Add them to your strengths list.

The Importance of Meaning

Another critical aspect to consider when searching for your True Self strengths is *meaning*. Jobs that provide meaning to our lives have a tremendous impact on joy. A meaningful job provides a deep sense of purpose and fulfillment. It can enable you to feel like you can make a real impact in the world.

Meaning can be found in all types of jobs—the school janitor, who finds meaning in providing a clean environment for children to grow and learn; the scientist, who is working on a cure for cancer; the consultant, who wants to help clients find the best versions of themselves. Meaning is created by the individual, not the job, and can often signify the difference between a "job," a "career," and a "calling."

A study from Wharton Business School demonstrated that we experience up to three times higher levels of motivation, engagement, and productivity when our work is meaningful.[iv] Additionally, researchers at Mount Sinai St Luke's and Mount Sinai Roosevelt reviewed 10 relevant studies of more than 137,000 people to determine the impact of purpose on death rates and risk of cardiovascular events. The analysis found that a high sense of purpose is associated with a 19% reduced risk of heart attack, stroke, or heart surgery and a 23% reduction in death from all causes.[v] These studies show that finding meaning in your work is an important contributor to joy, as well as to overall health.

Strengths + Contexts + Meaning = Joy

What meaning do you find from using your strengths? Look

at your list of strengths and associated contexts and attribute meaning where appropriate.

For example, Jennifer is a consultant who teaches sales in the legal industry. She works with lawyers in some of the largest law firms in the world to help them develop their business and secure new clients. When asked once why she worked in this industry—what meaning she found—her response was, "There are so many bad jokes about lawyers that there is the perception that they are un-lovable. I want to help them become lovable. I want to help them tap into their relationship-building skills to land clients who can't imagine a world without them."

At this point, you have a list of your True Self strengths, contexts, and meaning. Now you will look at how much *time* you currently spend utilizing those strengths.

Step Six: Diarize the Time Spent Within Your Strengths

How often do you get to engage in your True Self strengths? For one or two of your more typical weeks at work, engage in a time study.

At the end of each day, reflect on what you did that day. Look at your day in 15-minute increments to ascertain what activities or tasks you engaged in. For each activity or task, rate your invigo-ration level on a scale of 1–3, where 1 is highly invigorating and 3 is not at all invigorating. Here is a sample spreadsheet that you could start for yourself.

	Monday		Tuesday		Wednesday	
9:00	Triaged email	3	Triaged email	3	Triaged email	3
9:15	Wrote memo to the team	2	Difficult conversation with a team member	3	Worked on new process for Project X	1
9:30	Attended a brainstorming session for Project X	1	Same as above	3	Called customer Y re: their questions	2
9:45	Same as above	1	Documented difficult conversation	3	Same as above	2

At the end of the week, ask yourself the following questions:

- What percentage of my time did I spend in activities or tasks that rate a '1'?
  - ◊ Which strengths did I leverage during this time?
  - ◊ How did I feel during these times?

- What percentage of my time did I spend in activities or tasks that rate a '3'?
  - ◊ Which of my skills that I don't enjoy did I have to use during these times?
  - ◊ How did I feel during these times?

Likely, when you were engaged in level '1' tasks, you felt capable, in control, strong, and confident. The goal is to increase the amount of overall time, as much as reasonably possible, spent in your level '1' activities. In this way, you will regularly use the strengths that bring you joy.

Some of the level '3' activities may have involved your weaknesses or skills that you don't enjoy. Both can be active in your jobs. You likely already have an awareness of these and didn't necessarily need a time study to tell you what tasks you don't like.

While you were doing those activities, you were probably thinking about when you'd be able to stop. You weren't interested in improving. You were bored or struggled to concentrate. You certainly didn't volunteer for the work. Time seemed to crawl by when you had to do it.

These are all clues for activities that don't align with your True Self strengths. There is a school of thought that to achieve success you should work to improve your weaknesses. However, even when you improve in your weak areas, if they don't invigorate you, they can still sabotage your joy.

You need to try to minimize the time and energy spent in those activities. Focus on your highest and most invigorating strengths. Work to improve those and spend as much time as you can working within them.

Step Seven: Craft Your Job to Your Strengths

We know two things for sure about joy and strengths. You have to know what you do best, and you have to find the best fit between your strengths and your job. Certainly, thinking about your strengths will not be a new concept to you. Most of us have understood enough about what makes us happy at work to find jobs that call on aspects of our strengths. But to be a Joychiever, you need to find ways to make the best part of your job the biggest part of your job.

In some circumstances, you may face some challenges in achieving this if:

- You accepted the position out of necessity—it was your only option at the time, it provides a steppingstone to a better role, or the pay was incredibly attractive.

- You didn't have a clear enough understanding of all aspects of the job when you accepted it. Now you spend more time in activities that drain you, rather than invigorate you.

- The role or your employer's priorities have changed over time and you needed to change, too, in order to keep your job.

- You are part of a team and your strengths don't align with what the team needs most to be successful. You don't want to rock the boat, so you do what is asked of you.

Here are some ways to increase the amount of time that you spend working within your strengths:

- Look for missed or new opportunities to leverage your strengths in your current role. For example, if meeting facilitation is a strength, could you volunteer to run the team meetings more often?

- Seek training to further develop your strengths. For example, if you want to handle more negotiations with clients, could you request higher levels of training to become an expert negotiator on the team?

- Ask others to mentor you. If you want to rise in management because you have good people skills, can you ask more senior people to give you advice and guidance in order to achieve this goal?

- Ask other team members to take on the tasks that don't invigorate you. Those tasks may be strengths for them.

- Let your boss know your strengths and collaboratively work to structure your job towards those strengths. Ask her if she can direct appropriate assignments your way.

- Look for new situations where you could use your strengths. If there is a new cross-departmental project that would let you use your strategic planning skills, raise your hand to be on the team.

- Shadow a team member who shares one of your strengths. See how he is using those strengths on a more regular basis.

Of course, there will always be some activities that you can't drop and need to continue to do, but regularly ask yourself:

"How can I lean into my strengths more today, this week or this month?"

Summary

Given that we spend one-third of our lives working, Joychievers need to take steps to use their True Self strengths as often as they can. Let these seven steps guide your assessment of your strengths for clarity.

1. Think about what talents come naturally.
2. Ask others about your strengths.
3. Reflect on your crowning moments.
4. Capture your specific strengths.
5. Explore best-fit contexts.
6. Diarize the time spent within your strengths.
7. Craft your job to your strengths.

Endnotes

i   Buckingham, Marcus. *Go Put Your Strengths to Work: 6 Powerful Steps to Achieve Outstanding Performance*. New York: Free Press, 2011. p.11.

ii   Ibid. p.15.

iii   "Personal Strengths & Weaknesses Defined (+ List of 92 Strengths)." PositivePsychology.com, April 06, 2020. Accessed April 24, 2020. https://positivepsychology.com/what-are-your-strengths/.

iv   Achor, Shawn. *Before Happiness: the 5 Hidden Keys to Achieving Success, Spreading Happiness, and Sustaining Positive Change*. New York: Crown Business, 2013. p.72.

v   "Heart health improved by sense of purpose." (March 10, 2015). Accessed July 24, 2020. https://www.medicalbrief.co.za/archives/heart-health-improved-by-sense-of-purpose/.

LEISURE COVE: ENJOY THE 9 BENEFITS OF PLAY

"It's impossible to live a rich and full life without doing things that give you joy. Forget about productivity once in a while and give yourself permission to goof off."

— *Amy Morin*

"Leisure? Hobbies? Yeah, right. Who has the time?"

This is a common response from overachievers when it comes to how to spend their free time. Yet leisure, or play, should be prized and nurtured just like any of the other areas on your journey. It's critical for you to have something that you enjoy outside of work and domestic responsibility.

Understandably, it may seem daunting to add ONE MORE THING to your day, but leisure, not surprisingly, has been shown to improve a positive mood, lessen a negative mood, lower stress, and lower your heart rate.[i]

The word leisure comes from the Latin word *licere*, meaning "to be permitted" or "to be free." The notion of leisure time is thought to have started during the Industrial Revolution in the late nineteenth century in Victorian Britain. Early factory workers typically worked six days a week with only Sunday off. The emergence of work efficiencies and trade unions eventually enabled workers to take Saturdays off as well, which led to the Victorian concept of "the weekend" and the idea of leisure time as it is known today.[ii]

Seppo Iso-Ahola, Professor of Sport Psychology at the University of Maryland, suggests that the reasons people participate in leisure lies across two dimensions—*escaping* and *seeking*. Leisure activities can provide an *escape* from the everyday routine, one's challenges and troubles, and the people you see every day. Leisure can provide relief from a person's constraining life, particularly work.

On the other hand, people may *seek* psychological and personal satisfaction from leisure. Personal satisfaction can involve a sense of competence, challenge, learning, exploration, and relaxation. Additionally, people may engage in leisure for social contact and a feeling of connectedness.[iii]

The US Bureau of Labor Statistics regularly conducts the American Time Use Survey, which provides interesting information about how Americans spend their time and, in this case, how leisure time is spent.[1]

- Employed men spend 3.86 hours of time in leisure activities on each weekday and 6.47 hours on each weekend day.

- Employed women spend 3.1 hours of time in leisure activities on each weekday and 5.39 hours on each weekend day.

Here's the breakdown for how that leisure time is spent (in order of time spent):

1　Leisure time does not include household activities, caring for family members, shopping, personal care, preparing meals, or education.

Men

1. Watching TV
2. Socializing
3. Playing games
4. Relaxing/thinking
5. Sports/exercise/ recreation
6. Computer use (no games)
7. Reading for personal interest

Women

1. Watching TV
2. Socializing
3. Relaxing/thinking
4. Sports/exercise/recreation
5. Reading for personal interest
6. Computer use (no games)
7. Playing games

Let me tell you about my friend, Jack, who has been a lifelong hobbyist. He is an owner and leader of his business, serves on a couple of charity boards, and is married with three children.

He pursues hobbies that are challenging, interesting, and quite involved. For the hobbies he has selected, he often thinks, "People do this...? If they can do this, *I* can do this!" He finds it extremely rewarding to set a bold goal for himself and then accomplish it. For example, one of his lifelong passions is shooting, mostly with bow and arrow but also with guns.

Jack was involved in hunting with guns when he was young and was then exposed to archery during college. He found the mechanics of the bow intriguing and more elegant than a gun. Jack discovered that when he shoots with a bow, whether on a range or when out hunting, he enters a meditative type of space. He clears his mind, is in the moment, and is completely focused on his target. He forgets about everything else.

Jack learned to shoot a target with a bow at a distance of 20 yards and eventually became competent at shooting a target at 40 yards. But he said, "Forty yards was a really big deal. It was hard!" Fifteen years later, he was invited to go on an elk hunt, but to participate he needed to be able to shoot a target at 60 yards with his bow. Jack practiced intensely for a month, working on his form and technique, in order to become competent. All that training paid off as he "harvested" an elk of a lifetime during that hunt.

Jack now has an archery range in his backyard (he has a large backyard) with targets up to 100 yards. He went from hitting targets at 60 to 100 yards almost immediately once he decided that he could. His range is his happy place. When Jack needs to relax and get out of his head, that is where he goes. Jack has had a similar experience with photography and is now learning how to make moonshine.

9 Benefits of Play

Making time for leisure activities is a critical component for becoming a Joychiever. Here's why.

1. Reduces stress

Leisure activities can help you to relax and take your mind off work, household work, and other responsibilities. They give you a mental escape and help you to avoid burnout. Hobbies can also provide some physical benefits. For example, research on knitting shows that it can lower your blood pressure and lower your heart rate by an average of 11 beats a minute.[iv] Additionally, 74% of knitters in a University of British Columbia study claimed that knitting was calming and therapeutic.[v]

Hobbies that can help to reduce stress can include listening to music, reading, stargazing, archery, birdwatching, knitting, pottery, or journaling.

2. Provides a sense of purpose or meaning

As we discussed with strengths, feeling drawn to something as a calling or purpose is an important factor for joy. We all want to have meaning, which can be defined as feeling like part of something that you believe is bigger than yourself.[vi] It provides an answer to the "why?" in your life.

Often, as an overachiever, you are so busy moving forward that when the end of the day or week comes, you are too exhausted to find the time to consider what gives your life meaning. If your work isn't providing meaning, look to your hobbies to help fill that cup.

As an added note, if you decide to volunteer to find meaning, you may help yourself to live longer. A study of people aged 55 and older who volunteer found a 44% reduction in early death.[vii]

If you are searching for more meaning or purpose in your life, try to spend time at a senior living facility, read books to children, foster animals, work on home improvement, serve meals at a soup kitchen, deliver meals on wheels, drive cancer patients to their medical appointments, or volunteer at church.

3. Makes you more interesting

Hobbies enable you to break away from the monotony of your daily schedule and avoid the repetitive cycle that can happen in the typical working week of an overachiever. Additionally, hobbies can give you experiences that you can share with others and, potentially, create a common ground or bond to help a relationship grow. They can also help to keep your relationship with your love partner vibrant.

To add more intrigue and interest to your life, you could travel, go backpacking, try outdoor treasure-hunting with a geocaching group, shop for antiques, collect records, or practice with at-home science experiments.

4. Explores your untapped talents

Leisure activities can help you to explore talents that you haven't yet had the opportunity to realize. They can push you out of your comfort zone to try something new without pressure. You may surprise yourself. For example, you might assume that you are not creative until you take an improv class that shows you otherwise. Additionally, if work doesn't allow you to use all your talents, hobbies can provide you with that outlet.

To explore your untapped talents, you could take classes in art or acting or lessons in music, cooking, or a foreign language.

5. Develops your strengths

Hobbies can be a great way to focus on strengths that you may need to improve upon for work. You can enjoy the process of developing a strength without worrying about perfection, like you would on the job. For example, you could join Toastmasters to practice your public-speaking skills or volunteer to lead a committee at church to improve your people-management skills. You could also take some continuing education classes at a local college or university.

If you would like to develop professional strengths in your leisure time, you could take accounting classes or training in IT. You could volunteer to be a docent to practice your public-speaking or plan events for a charity to work on your organization or people-management skills.

6. Vitalizes your brain

Leisure can keep your brain active and vibrant. Meditation and yoga can enable you to find a peaceful state, while craft hobbies, like sewing, can help improve your focus and memory. John Medina, in his book *Brain Rules for Aging Well,* shares that the speed at which your brain takes in, processes, and reacts to outside stimuli decreases as you age. He suggests video games as a way to keep the brain sharp.[viii]

To keep your brain youthful, try meditation, yoga, board/card/ app games, history exploration, collecting, trivia, chess, or puzzles.

7. Engages your social relationships

Hobbies are a great way to meet new people and share similar interests. Countless studies show that social connection is a key component to happiness. According to researchers, we all need about six hours of socializing [through work and hobbies] to have a good and fulfilled day.[ix] Additionally, socializing can expose you to varied opinions, different kinds of people, and other ways to look at life.

Try new restaurants, movies, board games, wine tasting, festivals, billiards, book clubs, weekly card games, or sporting leagues to increase interactivity with your friends or to find new friends with similar interests.

8. Keeps you fit

Spending time exercising has so many benefits for your brain and your body. Exercise releases endorphins, which help to combat cortisol and adrenaline from stress and can keep both your mind and body healthy and fit. Exercise can also provide challenge and reward, for example setting a goal and then running a marathon.

Hiking, swimming, running, martial arts, surfing, scuba diving, skiing, ice skating, and strength training are all good ways to work on your fitness.

9. Taps into your creativity

Leisure activities can provide an outlet for your creativity. You can leverage this creativity for the fun of it or to solve a problem at work. If you sit at a desk crunching numbers during the week, you could paint or garden on the weekends to provide balance. If you spend your day being physically challenged, such as standing all day, you can take up a hobby that is mentally challenging.

If you would like to expand your creative side, you could garden, paint, draw, cook, or write. You could also engage in photography, decorate cakes, make your own soap, play a musical instrument, or become an amateur mixologist.

Identifying a Hobby

Since this chapter is about leisure, let's play a game. Try to match the celebrity with the hobby in the list below.[2]

1.	Brad Pitt	a.	Playing saxophone
2.	Jennifer Garner	b.	Golf
3.	Lebron James	c.	Kitesurfing
4.	Jon Stewart	d.	Football
5.	Tom Hanks	e.	Collecting vintage typewriters
6.	Richard Branson	f.	Ping pong
7.	Justin Timberlake	g.	Pottery & knitting
8.	Gordon Ramsay	h.	Crossword puzzles
9.	Nick Offerman	i.	Collecting headbands
10.	Susan Sarandon	j.	Woodworking

If you don't have clarity about what would be fun for you or maybe it has been a long time since you have prioritized your leisure time, it might seem like an overwhelming task to figure out what hobbies you would like to take up. Consider the following questions to help give you some guidance:

- Do you prefer doing things alone or with others?
- Is there a skill you would like to develop?
- Do you need to find a way to relax?
- Is there something that you miss doing?
- How much time can you make available for a hobby?
- In what ways would you want a hobby to challenge you?

---

2   Answers to celebrity hobbies: 1. g, 2. a, 3. i, 4. h, 5. e, 6. c, 7. b, 8. d, 9. j, 10. f.

- Are you interested in being more physically active?
- With what types of people would you like to interact?
- What activity would easily bring a smile to your face?
- What activities make time disappear for you?

After thinking through the answers to these questions, you could start a leisure file. Collect notes about anything that grabs your attention—articles, pictures, random thoughts. What looks like fun? What would you like to find out more about? What would you like to try?

After a month or so, go through the file. Consider your time and resources and give one of your ideas a try. The good news is that your choice doesn't mean that you are wedded to it forever. Over time you can continue to work through all the ideas in your file.

Endnotes

i   Zawadzki, M. J., J. M. Smyth and H. J. Costigan. "Real-Time Associations Between Engaging in Leisure and Daily Health and Well-Being." *Annals of Behavioral Medicine*. (2015) *49*(4), 605–615. Accessed April 29, 2020. https://doi.org/10.1007/s12160-015-9694-3.

ii   "Leisure Time." Psychology Wiki. Accessed April 29, 2020. https://psychology.wikia.org/wiki/Leisure_time.

iii   Walker, Gordon J., Douglas A. Kleiber and Roger C. Mannell. *A Social Psychology of Leisure*. Urbana, IL: Sagamore-Venture, 2019.

iv   Knit for Peace. "The Health Benefits Of Knitting." Accessed April 29, 2020. https://www.knitforpeace.org.uk/wp-content/uploads/2017/05/The-Health-Benefits-of-Knitting-Preview.pdf.

v   Clave-Brule, M., A. Mazloum, R. J. Park, E. J. Harbottle and C. L. Birmingham. September 01, 2020. "Managing anxiety in eating disorders with knitting." Accessed May 01, 2020. https://pubmed.ncbi.nlm.nih.gov/19367130/.

vi   Seligman, Martin E. P. *Flourish: A Visionary New Understanding of Happiness and Well-Being*. New York: Atria, 2013.

vii   Oman, D., C. E. Thoresen and K. McMahon, "Volunteerism and Mortality Among the Community Dwelling Elderly." *Journal of Health Psychology*. (1999) *4*(3) 301–16. Accessed, May 22, 2020.https://pubmed.ncbi.nlm.nih.gov/22021599/.

viii   Medina, John, and Tracy Cutchlow. *Brain Rules for Aging Well: 10 Principles for Staying Vital, Happy, and Sharp*. Seattle, WA: Pear Press, 2017.

ix   "Is Social Connection a Path to Happiness? SimplyCircle Guest Post." SimplyCircle, September 4, 2018. Accessed May 01, 2020. https://simplycircle.com/social-connection-happiness/.

BODY BEACH: REVIVE, THRIVE AND BE ALIVE, BABY!

"Take care of your body. It's the only place you have to live."

— *Jim Rohn*

Welcome to Body Beach—one of the most critical True Self stops for Joychievers to explore. As an overachiever, you may take a well-functioning body for granted. You wake up in the morning and get moving, not necessarily thinking about how many things go right in your body every waking minute. When busy, stressed, or overwhelmed, you may even neglect your body by minimizing sleep, not exercising, eating improperly, or worse.

Without the body, there is no life. Spending time on Body Beach ensures your body functions at as optimal a level as possible. Multiple industries focus on the body—fitness, diet, specific health issues, and more, so we'll focus here on three areas critical to overachievers: stress, sleep, and exercise.

Stress

According to WebMD, 43% of all adults suffer adverse health effects from stress. In fact, 75%–90% of all doctors' office visits are for stress-related concerns, and stress costs American industry more than $300 billion a year. [i]

As an overachiever, stress can be a daily part of life. As a Joychiever, you must be vigilant about managing it. It's too easy to simply bounce from stress situation to stress situation, such as from work to home to work, without any break in between. Thankfully, the human body is designed to experience and react to stress.

There is good stress and bad stress.

Good stress—"eustress"—happens when you are engaged in an activity that may feel demanding but is also invigorating and exciting. The activity may also result in a positive outcome. Examples of eustress include getting a job promotion, buying a new home, having a child, or planning a vacation. Eustress is typically short term, can motivate and focus your energy, and feels manageable.

Bad stress—"distress"—happens in situations that cause continuous challenges and can have an unknown or negative outcome. Examples of distress can include losing your job, having health problems, experiencing conflict with an important person in your life, or financial worries. Distress can be short or long term, can paralyze your energy, and often feels unmanageable.

You need to manage both types of stress, but typically, when you hear about "stress management," people are mostly referring to the bad stress. It's the prolonged and chronic nature of distress that is most damaging to our bodies.

It's unreasonable to expect that you will never experience stress. The better strategy is to constantly be on the lookout for signs of it so that you can seek ways to give your body a break from its effects.

Here are some signs that stress might be getting the better of you:

On your body	On your mood	On your behavior
• Acne • Headache • Muscle tension • Fatigue • Insomnia • Upset stomach, diarrhea, or constipation • Pain • Hair loss • Change in sex drive • Rapid heartbeat • Chest pain	• Decreased energy • Anxiety • Feeling overwhelmed • Irritability • Constant worry • Sadness • Anger • Depression	• Emotional outbursts • Overeating • Undereating • Bad decisions • Drug or alcohol misuse • Smoking • Social withdrawal • Work performance issues • Thoughts of dangerous behavior to yourself or others

As an overachiever experiencing these signals, you may, 1) try to "power through," thinking they are temporary, 2) ignore these signs as "one-off" or inconsequential, 3) acknowledge the signs but not change your behavior, or 4) allow them to build up to the state of burnout or illness.

As I reflect on my "Lauren" life, I can say that I experienced 45% of those signs on a nearly constant basis towards the end. I kept making excuses like, "If I just get through the next week/month/ three months, things will calm down." Or "Yes, I'm stressed but isn't everybody?" Or "I love what I do. I can handle this!"

How many excuses have you made for your stress levels?

Any of these effects, over time, will lead to continued strain on your body. It would be as if you have your foot on the gas pedal and never take it off. That type of behavior can lead to serious health problems, such as heart disease, heart attack, high blood pressure, diabetes, and mental health disorders such as depression.

A Joychiever notices these signals and takes action to give the body a break—taking the foot off the gas pedal—enabling the body to rebalance itself and return optimal functionality.

There are hundreds of resources that offer stress management techniques. Here are a few that may be a help for you:

- **Create boundaries.** If work is your primary stressor, keep it contained. Don't let work bleed into your home or social time. Set rules for yourself about when and how you will respond to work messages (and respect those rules). If you must work at home during the evenings or on the weekend, set specific appointments for yourself and work with focus and efficiency.

- **Take a break from technology.** For many overachievers, smartphones have become an additional appendage. From time to time, step away from your smartphone, your computer, and other technology devices. If you don't, it's too tempting to check work messages or the news, which makes it impossible get away from sources of stress.

- **Talk it out.** Lean into your family, friends, coach, or therapist as outlets for your stress. With someone you trust, discuss what is stressing you, both to get it off your chest and to hear an additional perspective.

- **Find time for you.** Depending on your situation, work and home might both be sources of stress for you. It's critical that you find time just for you, to get away from it all, and to clear your head and recharge. Even if it's a 10-minute walk around the block, seek those moments for yourself.

- **Engage in exercise/meditation/yoga.** Exercise, mediation, and yoga release endorphins and dopamine and strengthen the connection between the prefrontal cortex and the amygdala. Exercise and yoga also help you to stay fit.

- **Laugh.** Laughter can reduce cortisol and adrenaline and release dopamine, the "pleasure hormone." Find people, movies, books, videos, etc. that make you laugh and give yourself a full dose of laughter.

- **Take a vacation.** You deserve a break. You *need* a break to continue to perform at optimal levels. Even Olympic athletes focus on their recovery so they don't overtrain to negative effect. Don't skip vacation; avoid work while on vacation; and start planning your next vacation on the day you return home.

Sleep

Do you know that you have access to an "elixir of life" that you could start using tonight?

This elixir can lengthen your life, ward off illness, and keep you slim. Studies show it enhances your memory and could protect you from cancer and dementia. It lowers your risk of heart attacks and diabetes. You feel happier and even look more attractive upon taking it.

Who wouldn't want this elixir? It sounds amazing. Yet overachievers often take pride in how little of this elixir they utilize in their lives. And when you admit to having some, others sometimes make you feel guilty for indulging, as if you are weak or lazy.

This elixir of life is SLEEP.

The world is facing a sleep deprivation epidemic. In the US and Canada, for example, 30% of people are regularly sleeping six hours or less a night. There is even a World Sleep Day, which began in 2007, to celebrate sleep and create a call to action for sleep issues. (In case you're interested, it occurs on the Friday before the Spring Vernal Equinox every year.)

It's time for you Joychiever to reclaim your right to sleep because if you don't, insufficient sleep *will* kill you.

There are over 17,000 scientific reports from around the world that corroborate this claim. Here are just a few:[ii]

- A 2011 study of more than half a million men and women of varied ages and ethnicities across eight different countries showed that shorter sleep was associated with a 45% increased risk of developing and/or dying from coronary heart disease.
- Another study of adults aged 45 or older who sleep fewer than six hours a night are 200% more likely to have a heart attack or stroke during their lifetime.
- A large European study of almost 25,000 individuals demonstrated that sleeping six hours or less a night was associated with a 40% increased risk of developing cancer.
- A study compared drowsy drivers and drunk drivers using a driving simulator. Participants who had four hours of sleep and no alcohol had the same number of driving errors as participants who slept eight hours and were legally drunk. And participants who had both four hours of sleep and were legally drunk saw a 500% increase in driving errors.
- In the US, a car accident caused by sleeplessness occurs every 30 seconds and exceeds those caused by alcohol and drugs combined.
- In a 10-day study where participants slept for five to six hours each night, they consumed 300 additional calories a

day, which over a year equates to 70,000 extra calories or 10 to 15 lbs.

- In a study looking at the relationship between sleep and the common cold, participants who slept five hours on average every night for a week before being injected with a cold virus had a 50% infection rate. Those who slept seven hours or more a night incurred only an 18% infection rate.

- In studies on beauty sleep, one experiment showed that sleep-deprived faces look more weary with redder and more swollen eyes, dark under-eye circles, more wrinkles, and droopier eyelids.[iii] A second study found that those who didn't sleep well exhibited more signs of skin aging including fine lines, uneven pigmentation, and reduced skin elasticity.[iv]

Have I convinced you yet?

Are you persuaded to trade in the badge of honor that many over-achievers wear because of their ability to function without sleep for one of a prolific sleeper?

In case you need a little more convincing, how about this: Every major system, tissue, and organ of your body suffers when sleep becomes short. Insufficient sleep has causal relationships with heart disease, obesity, diabetes, dementia, and cancer. It can even alter DNA. It is also linked to Alzheimer's disease, anxiety, depression, bipolar disorder, suicide, stroke, and chronic pain.[v]

When you think of insufficient sleep, you likely think of pulling all-nighters or nights where you may get less than four or five hours of sleep. In reality, even six hours of sleep constitutes a sleep deficiency. With seven to nine hours of sleep being the recommendation, even one hour of less sleep can have an impact.

Look at daylight saving time—the human-instituted practice of losing one hour in the spring and gaining an hour in the fall.

A 2014 study shows a 25% jump in the number of heart attacks occurring on the Monday after daylight saving time began.[vi] There is a comparable decrease in the fall when we gain the hour when daylight saving time ends. Similar effects have been reported for car accidents and strokes at those times of the year.

So how do you know if you're getting enough sleep? Ask yourself two questions. First, after waking up in the morning, do you feel the need to take a nap by 10:00 or 11:00 a.m.? Second, do you need caffeine to function well before noon? If the answer is "yes" to either or both questions, you are likely not getting enough sleep or are lacking in quality sleep.[vii]

Unfortunately, what happens over time is that you acclimatize to your sleep-deprived state. Lower alertness, reduced energy, increased need for caffeine, and decreased performance become the norm. It also starts you on the slow road to poor health, compromised mental aptitude, and even death.

To get sleep working to your advantage, you need to **focus on quantity, quality, and regularity**. You need more than seven hours to maintain optimal performance physically, mentally, and emotionally. Here are 12 tips for good sleep:[viii]

1. **Stick to a sleep schedule.** If you adopt any of these tips, focus on this one. It has the biggest impact on better sleep. Go to bed and wake up at the same time every day, even on the weekend. We are creatures of habit and have a difficult time adjusting to changes in sleep patterns, even if they are small.

2. **Exercise.** Exercise can help you to feel tired at night but don't exercise two to three hours before bedtime. It can wind up your energy and make it difficult to fall asleep.

3. **Avoid caffeine, especially in the afternoons or evenings.**
   Caffeine attaches to the same receptors that receive adenosine, a chemical in your brain that promotes sleep. As
   caffeine can last for 10–14 hours in your system, it essentially blocks adenosine from doing its job, making it difficult for you to fall asleep.

4. **Avoid alcohol before bed.** Alcohol robs you of REM sleep
   and may impair your breathing during the night. Plus,
   your snoring may have the added impact of waking up
   your partner.

5. **Avoid large meals and beverages closer to bedtime.** A
   large meal can cause indigestion, and too many fluids may
   create the urge to run to the bathroom throughout the
   night. Conversely, don't go to bed extremely hungry. It can
   also keep you awake.

6. **Don't nap after 3:00 p.m.** A brief nap can help you get
   through the day, but if you sleep too late in the day, it can
   make it harder to fall asleep at night.

7. **Unwind before bed.** Find a relaxing activity to help your
   mind disengage from the day and prepare for rest and recovery.

8. **Cool your bedroom.** Your body temperature increases
   throughout the day and begins to decrease in mid-after-
   noon. It continues to decrease until 5:00 a.m., while you
   are sleeping. A cool bedroom, 65°F/18°C, will help you to
   fall asleep and stay asleep.

9. **Darken your room.** Your circadian rhythm is driven by
   light. If you have lights on in your room or don't block the
   outside light, it can wreak havoc on its cycle. Your body
   may think it's time to wake up when it's actually time to
   sleep.

10. **Minimize electronics.** Technology in the bedroom can create bad habits that are detrimental to sleep. They are too tempting to use or check during the night, which perks up your brain. Additionally, exposure to blue light from electronics can interfere with your circadian rhythm and melatonin release, which negatively impacts your sleep. If you must have a phone in your room, turn off all sounds and develop habits to avoid checking it throughout the night.

11. **Have the right daylight exposure.** Daylight is key to regulating daily sleep patterns. Try to get outside in natural sunlight for at least 30 minutes each day and turn down the lights before bedtime.

12. **Don't lie in bed awake.** If you find yourself still awake for more than 20 minutes, get up and do some relaxing activity until you feel sleepy. Also, try to avoid looking at the clock. The anxiety of watching time tick by while not being able to sleep can make it harder to fall back to sleep.

You have to find a combination of techniques that work for you. I utilize a number of these suggestions. My husband likes to tease me because I am very particular about staging our bedroom for sleep. It has to be very dark—blinds are blackout and no light can emit from any of the electronics that may be charging overnight, it has to be quiet—except for a fan set low for ambient noise and it has to be cold.

That setup has long been a habit for me. However, recently, I have been working diligently to stick to a sleep schedule. Yes, that means that I go to bed a little earlier on the weekends, typically around 10:00 p.m., but it has had the biggest positive impact on my quality and quantity of sleep. On the days when I go to bed later, I get a second wind in the evening and then can't fall asleep until well after midnight, and my sleep doesn't feel as deep or as restful. When I stick to the schedule, I sleep solidly and feel great the next day.

So go on, try some of these techniques tonight and enjoy the elixir.

Exercise

I wish I had a penny for every article or news story that has ever been shared about exercise and its benefits. I would be rich many times over. Yet less than 5% of adults participate in 30 minutes of physical activity each day, and only 30% of adults achieve the recommended amount of physical activity each week. Even more disturbing is that one in six US adults and children are obese, and by 2030, half of all adults in the US will be obese, according to the President's Council on Sports, Fitness, and Nutrition.[ix]

Now I could turn on the guilt and shame engine and overwhelm you with more statistics to scare you or list numerous benefits to try to lure you to exercise, but likely you already know many of them. My only interest, however, is in helping you to find the time to exercise regularly, with the key word here being "regularly."

Many of you may exercise already. Bravo! But for many over-achievers, exercise is often one of the first activities that falls off the list when we get busy, overwhelmed, or stressed. Instead, it needs to go to the top of the list. After sleep, exercise is the next best thing you can do for your body and your mind, and it's a great way to ensure you find joy.

Consider the following questions to help you find your path to exercise.

How much exercise makes an impact?

First, know that any movement helps. For those of us with office jobs and commutes, we often sit for a good part of the day. The key is to sit less and move more. Instead of the elevator, take the stairs to a meeting. Secure a stand-up desk. If possible, take some of your meetings standing up or walking around the block.

In 2018, the Office of Disease Prevention and Health Promotion within the US Department of Health released the new Physical Activity Guidelines. This is their infographic.[x]

It has long been the recommendation to do 150 minutes a week of moderate-intensity aerobic activity. Now the US Department of Health is incorporating strength training, as well as higher intensity exercise. Ideally, exercise should comprise 150–300 minutes of moderate activity or 75–150 minutes of vigorous activity, plus strength-training twice a week.

What kind of exercise is optimal?

To figure out which aerobic exercise works best for you, first focus on the intensity level of the exercise, which you can determine using the Talk Test. If you can still have a conversation easily while exercising, it's probably a moderate-intensity exercise. These activities can include brisk walking, cycling, snow shoveling by hand, or playing in the yard with your children. If you can only say a few words before needing a breath, it's probably a vigorous-intensity exercise. These activities can include running, climbing stairs, digging in your garden, or fast-paced dancing.

Given your fitness level and interests, determine which intensity level would work for you. If you don't currently exercise, I wouldn't recommend starting with 30 minutes of running, for example (even if you used to be able to run easily in the past). You may hurt yourself or, just as importantly, you may feel like a failure because you won't be able to complete the run. Find what can work for you in your current state and build gradually to higher levels of fitness.

Remember it's also important to work in muscle-strengthening activities, such as resistance training, body weight exercises, and weightlifting, as recommended. Strength training increases bone density, boosts your metabolism, and keeps you looking fit.

How do I find the time?

Finding specific times to work out during a week may seem impossible but try these tips for fitting exercise into your busy routine.

- **Count what you're already doing.** For example, some household activities, such as cleaning, playing with children, and walking the dog can add up towards the recommended guideline, if they are vigorous enough.

- **Add exercise into other activities.** Spend time with family in a park. Catch up with your spouse over a run. Invite a client to spin class instead of to dinner.

- **Leverage technology.** There is a plethora of apps and trackers that can monitor your activity and help you stay motivated.

- **Focus on vigorous-intensity exercise.** The recommended guideline is cut in half if you can get your heart pumping faster. It may be easier to fit in 15 minutes of vigorous activity than 30 minutes of moderate activity five times a week.

- **Appreciate and reward your efforts.** If you can only exercise for 30 minutes a week, then that's better than nothing. See if you can do 30 minutes consistently every week and try to work that up to 40, 45, or even 60 minutes.

The key is to move and keep moving.

Exercise has been the key to my whole survival. From back when I was a young athlete, the need and enjoyment I gained from exercise has always stuck with me. That said, there have been times when I have been stressed, busy, or uninterested in working out but have still managed to find exercise apps with a choice of short, 15–20 minutes workouts. I tell myself that I can do anything for 15 minutes; I put on my exercise clothes and get it done. I *always* feel better after a workout.

Body Beach is the place for you to focus on getting the machine called your body functioning and well-tuned. Without it, there is no journey. While this chapter provides ideas to de-stress, recharge with sleep and fit healthy exercise into your routine, you may also need to focus on diet and other health issues that impact your body. Be loving and proactive will impact your physical joy.

Endnotes

i "The Effects of Stress on Your Body." WebMD, December 10, 2017. Accessed May 08, 2020. https://www.webmd.com/balance/stress-management/effects-of-stress-on-your-body.

ii Walker, Matthew P. Why We Sleep: Unlocking the Power of Sleep and Dreams. New York, NY: Scribner, an imprint of Simon & Schuster, 2018.

iii "Sleep Deprivation Affects Face Appearance, Study Shows." HuffPost, August 30, 2013. Accessed May 11, 2020. https://www.huffpost.com/entry/sleep-deprivation-face-appearance-ugly_n_3843913?guccounter=1&guce_referrer=aHR0cHM6Ly9zZWFyY2gueWFob28uY29tLw&guce_referrer_sig=AQAAAC-Q9UxTsYZSIYuSx7SjQBHPx-xGnUGVS7JKQTfZsA-uvAZhA76_lEAqb6uXB_f8irubJAFeBU2NEi-ELfmv1-YmnIWWmTzDLXb0W-tD3IXqO5weQX6tAKS-GYE9W_02q3m3YEWUO4ag3AiR1FpfAFVw2HNmohkxloG48b3QdSd7iY.

iv Emling, Shelley. "Here's Yet Another Important Reason To Get Enough Shut-Eye." HuffPost, July 24, 2013. Accessed May 11, 2020. https://www.huffpost.com/entry/sleep-deprivation-effects-aging-skin_n_3644269.

v Walker, Matthew P. Why We Sleep: Unlocking the Power of Sleep and Dreams. New York, NY: Scribner, an imprint of Simon & Schuster, 2018.

vi MacMillan, Amanda. "7 Ways Daylight Saving Time Can Affect Your Health." Health.com, March 10, 2019. Accessed May 12, 2020. https://www.health.com/condition/sleep/daylight-saving-time-health-risks.

vii Walker, Matthew P. Why We Sleep: Unlocking the Power of Sleep and Dreams. New York, NY: Scribner, an imprint of Simon & Schuster, 2018. p.35.

viii National Institutes of Health. "Your Guide to Healthy Sleep." Accessed July 23, 2020. https://www.nhlbi.nih.gov/files/docs/public/sleep/healthy_sleep.pdf.

ix HHS Office, and President's Council on Sports, Fitness, and Nutrition. "Facts & Statistics." HHS.gov, January 26, 2017. Accessed May 13, 2020. https://www.hhs.gov/fitness/resource-center/facts-and-statistics/index.html.

x Health.gov. "Walk. Run. Dance. Play. What's Your Move?" MoveYourWay. Accessed May 13, 2020. https://health.gov/moveyourway.

RELATIONSHIPS HARBOR: DISCOVER THE #1 SECRET TO HEALTHY AGING

"A friend is a gift you give yourself."

— *Robert Louis Stevenson*

Relationships are a key driver for joy. Some even say they're the secret to a happy and healthy life.

The Harvard Study of Adult Development has been following 724 males since 1938. It's the longest running study of its kind. Annually, the participants respond to questionnaires about their work, home lives, and health. They also provide medical records and blood samples, have their brains scanned, and allow researchers to talk to their children.

Upon closely examining the data, Dr. Robert Waldinger, the fourth director of the study, says, "The clearest message that we get from this study is this: Good relationships keep us happier and healthier. Period. It turns out that people who are more socially connected to family, to friends, to community are happier; they're physically healthier and they live longer than people who are less well connected."[i]

Specifically, relationships:

- Increase your sense of belonging and purpose.
- Boost your happiness.
- Reduce your stress and cortisol.
- Improve your self-confidence.
- Help you cope with adversity.

The challenge for overachievers is that we often feel we don't have time for relationships or, because we are so overwhelmed, we may retreat into ourselves. We miss the opportunity for relationships to help us through these stressful times and provide an outlet for joy.

You will have many types of relationships in your life. In this case, I'm referring to friendships and, specifically, to "inner-circle" friendships. Those people with whom you *choose* to spend your time and are closest to you.

Some relationships last for your whole life, and some are brief. With some friends, you share a deep connection; with others you may share certain interests. A few relationships reach best-friend status, and sometimes you hold on to relationships that should have expired years earlier.

This is why I'm using the concept of a "harbor" to discuss relationships. Boats come into dock—some for extended periods and some for brief periods, and both situations are okay. Some people are only meant to be in your life during certain times or as part of a set of circumstances. That is the ebb and flow of life.

What I find interesting is that we don't evaluate friendships in the same way as romantic relationships.

In romantic relationships, people may create a list of the characteristics of a perfect mate. Why isn't there as much thought and transparency around ideal friendships? Could we find more joy in our relationships if we did think about these things?

Components of Great Relationships

You will no doubt have some relationships that are joy-inducing and some that are joy-robbing. Joychievers try to surround themselves with more joy-inducing relationships. Here are seven components that can lead you to a joyful friendship.

While reading through the components, think of each of your "inner-circle" relationships in turn and rate that relationship where it falls along the joy-robbing/joy-inducing dimension. Please recognize that this is not a scientific survey. It's simply meant to give you an overall view of your relationship.

Values & Goals

Have you ever felt like you just "clicked" with someone? If so, it's highly likely that you share similar values and goals. In some cases, opposites can attract, but when it comes to values in great relationships, they are typically shared or complementary. Having opposing values can easily create conflict. In the same way, friendships can be formed when you share similar goals. Together, you can discuss ways to reach your goals, interesting moments along the journey, and how to overcome obstacles along the path.

Joy-robbing   1...........2...........3...........4...........5   Joy-inducing

Shared Interests

Like values and goals, relationships provide joy when you share similar or the same interests. Sharing hobbies or activities with a buddy can make them more fun. Whether it's yoga, travel, food, or music, you have someone with whom you can get out, do things together, and enjoy new experiences.

Joy-robbing　1...........2...........3...........4...........5　Joy-inducing

Generosity & Celebration

Choose friends who are generous with their energy, thoughtfulness, and celebration of you and your successes. A great friend will do the little things for you—send a note, just because, stock their fridge with your favorite beverage when you visit, or buy you the perfect birthday present—and be the first to say "congratulations!" for milestones and accomplishments along your journey.

Joy-robbing　1...........2...........3...........4...........5　Joy-inducing

Motivation, Encouragement & Growth

You want friends who strengthen, motivate, and encourage you. They help you to become the best version of yourself. Some friends may also balance their strengths with your weaknesses so that you can tap into their talents and wisdom as you grow. Great friends push you over the finish line, providing encouragement when you think you can't take another step.

Joy-robbing　1...........2...........3...........4...........5　Joy-inducing

Conflict Resolution

Conflict or disagreement happens in great relationships. What matters is how those conflicts are handled. Healthy conflict resolution involves listening to each other's needs, accepting the other person's opinion, and prioritizing the relationship to find an agreeable outcome. As a result of candid communication, healthy relationships don't let underlying tensions fester and linger.

Joy-robbing 1...........2...........3...........4...........5 Joy-inducing

Time & Effort

In a healthy relationship, each friend is happy with the amount of time that is put into the relationship. You may see each other regularly or you may not. Either way, the pace and frequency of connection works for you both. Good friends also understand that you may have other relationships or commitments and they don't make you feel guilty when you spend time in those areas. Conversely, the other person doesn't make you feel neglected or ignored if they are busy.

Joy-robbing   1...........2...........3...........4...........5 Joy-inducing

Life Stage & Frequency

Sharing a life stage or spending a lot of time with a person can help fuel a relationship. If both of you have a young family or are empty nesters, you may naturally have more in common. If you are neighbors or work together, whether down the hall from each other or virtually, it can be easier to invest time to nurture the relationship. This does not mean that you can't or shouldn't maintain a relationship if you are in different life stages or connect less frequently. It just may take a little more effort to keep it going.

Joy-robbing   1...........2...........3...........4...........5 Joy-inducing

If you have rated a relationship for all seven components, here's how to interpret the score.

If Your Total Is Above 25

If your score is higher than 25, this is a great relationship for you. You have many things in common, and this relationship is a regular source of support, fun, and encouragement. You look forward to the times when you can connect with this friend, and you enjoy supporting his or her journey, as well.

Relationships in this category need a strong foundation. For this to be an inner-circle, joy-inducing relationship for you, you have to invest time in it at some point. If frequency is enabled or proximity is shared, this can happen quite easily.

Long-term friendships often happen this way, where you share time with someone and develop the friendship. Then, for example, one of you may move away but because the foundation is secure, you can still enjoy the friendship because you have that base of experiences to rely upon.

I have this kind of experience with one of my long-term relationships. We met when I started a new job in 2000. She was my peer, and our offices were next door to each other. We hit it off instantly, and she was my best friend at work.

Work has always been the cornerstone for bringing us together. In 2002, she left for another company, and a year later, I followed her there. In 2006, I became a consultant, and she has hired me frequently since then. These work moments have given us opportunities to see each other, despite living in different cities for many years.

Our relationship receives 5's for all but the Life Stage & Frequency dimensions. I would love to be around her more, but it isn't feasible to make that happen in our lives right now. That said, when we do talk or get together, it's as if we saw each other yesterday. I know that if I called her in a crisis in need of help, she would drop everything to help me.

If Your Total Is Below 14

If your score is below 14 for any of your relationships, you may want to seriously consider the viability of the friendship. It's likely that this relationship is more joy-robbing than joy-inducing. Relationships may reach this level in a variety of ways. For example:

- The relationship may be a 5 in one or two dimensions but low in all others. The one high-scoring scale may have fulfilled a need for a particular period of time but over the months or years, the weight of the lower dimensions makes it joy-robbing.

  I used to have a friend like this. We met at a friend's party, and we seemed to have a lot in common. I was single and needed a social buddy because many of my friends were consumed with new husbands or new babies at the time. She was in a similar place so we started to do a lot of things together. After six months, I realized that the only thing that connected us was our socializing interest and the friendship faded quickly after that. Upon reflection, I am okay with it. I think we each filled a need for each other at that point in our lives and that was all we were meant to be.

- The relationship may not score well in any dimension but for other reasons, you keep this person around. There may be extenuating circumstances that you can't change or you see some glimmer of hope that keeps you going. However, if others question why you are friends or if you continuously make excuses for this person, you may want to reevaluate the friendship. Additionally, if this person doesn't treat you well, then it may be time to end it.

If Your Total Is Between 15 and 24

Relationships in the "middle" can be tough to navigate. In some areas, you two work really well together, and there is a lot of enjoyment. In other areas, it can be quite a struggle. These types of relationships tend to require a lot of effort to keep them in the joy-inducing range.

I had one relationship in particular for several years that lived in the middle, although I was unaware of this at the time. When our friendship started, I would have given us 5's across the board. We seemed to share interests, values, and goals and were "there" for each other during the ups and downs of our individual lives. We shared a number of fun experiences together and socialized at least once a week.

After time, however, I realized that some of those 5's were, in reality, much lower. While we shared similar life goals, our values weren't actually aligned. She could be very generous but only when she thought to be so. She didn't always support me in the ways that I needed or wanted and, regularly, she could take a day or two to respond to my messages. For a long time, I was okay with it. She didn't overtly treat me badly, but yet the relationship could have been more consistent on the joy front.

I talk about this relationship in the past tense because it did eventually fade away. I moved to another city so the frequency of our interaction dwindled. Plus, the effort scale was lopsided. I was extending a lot of effort and not receiving consistent friendship behavior in return. I was no longer willing to make those investments and felt comfortable that the relationship had run its course.

In general, the components of a great friendship are intended to be a source of introspection. Some of you may appreciate the idea of rating your relationships to gain more clarity about how your friendships are working for you. Others may feel that it demeans your relationships to put them into black and white on a piece of paper. That is not the intention. In our quest to choose joy daily, these components are humbly intended as a mere guide along that journey.

Tough Conversations

There are times in all relationships when you need to have tough conversations. They may be when you have to resolve a conflict or when you want to end a relationship. Healthy relationships have disagreements and engage in collaborative discussions to reach agreeable outcomes and understanding. Here are some techniques to help you through those discussions.

Conflict Resolution

When dealing with conflict in a relationship, there are two concepts that you can leverage to get to resolution:

1. Interests vs. Positions

Interests vs. positions is a classic negotiation strategy that works well in any relationship. By aiming to uncover and focus on interests, you can get to the heart of the matter and address both parties' greatest concerns. The challenge is that you often get caught up in the positions, and emotions can spin the conversation into an argument.

The long-used story to demonstrate how to use the concept is about two sisters fighting over the last orange on Earth.

> Pleading her case, Sister 1 said, "I deserve the orange because I worked hard over the last year."
>
> "I deserve it because I got better grades," replied Sister 2 defensively.
>
> "Well, I should have it because I will put it to better use," countered Sister 1.
>
> "Yeah, well, I cook better than you," harrumphed Sister 2.

And it could go on and on with each sister stating more "positions" for deserving the orange. They will likely never reach an agreement that satisfies them both.

What they don't realize is that if either of them had asked "Why" the other wanted the orange, they would have realized that one sister wanted the pulp of the orange for juice and the other wanted the rind for baking.

So often, when we are in disagreements, we get too focused in or stuck on our positions, rather than getting to our real interest. The key is to ask questions after the initial statement and to keep asking questions until you get to the heart of the matter. For example, here is a conversation that focuses on positions, not interests.

> Amy and Liz sat together for coffee one morning, as they regularly do, when Amy said something out of the blue.
>
> "I wish you liked to exercise more," Amy said.
>
> "I do like exercising," Liz replied. "I take walks."
>
> "Is walking exercise?"
>
> "It feels like exercise to me. I take walks around the neighborhood once or twice a week," Liz said. She was starting to feel defensive. Was Amy saying she needed to lose weight? Liz was surprised her friend would say something like that to her.
>
> "But you're not doing anything to improve your flexibility."
>
> "Well, what do you do?"
>
> "Not enough, that's the point! I want to exercise more," Amy said. She'd been thinking about joining a yoga class, but she didn't want to go alone. She knew that wasn't something Liz was usually interested in.
>
> "Well, why didn't you just say so!" Liz said, feeling confused at what Amy was trying to communicate.

What's interesting in this conversation is that the two friends get caught up in what constitutes "exercise" and find themselves in defensive positions and going round in a circle. What you will see in the next conversation, which uses questions to uncover interests, is that Amy really wants to try yoga, but this point is completely missed in their positions-oriented conversation.

"I wish you liked to exercise more," Amy said.

"I like to exercise, but what do you mean when you say 'exercise more?'" replied Liz, curious where Amy might be heading with the conversation.

"Well, I know you like to take walks, but I wish you wanted to do other things," Amy said in a hopeful tone.

"Yes, walking works for me," Liz said, "but I'd be open to other types of exercise. What interests you?" She was intrigued.

"Well, I was thinking about taking up yoga," Amy replied.

"Why yoga?" asked Liz.

"I need to work on my flexibility," Amy said. Lately, her muscles were feeling tight and had been struggling with her regular exercise routine.

"Hmm, I could work on my flexibility too. Have you looked into classes?" asked Liz.

"Yes, there are loads of options for studios or online classes, but I don't want to do it alone. It would be fun to share it with you," Amy said with a smile.

"Actually, that would be fun. I've never tried yoga. We could probably have a lot of laughs trying to get ourselves into those poses," Liz laughed.

"Exactly. Going to a class with people who already know how to do yoga intimidates me," Amy said.

"I get that. I guess I'd be willing to give it a try. Why don't we try a few online classes to get our feet wet and then we can look for a studio class," suggested Liz.

"Yes! That would be great!" Amy beamed.

Ultimately, Amy wanted to improve her flexibility and was looking to try a new exercise that intimidated her. She was hoping Liz could join her to make it less scary and more fun. By asking questions, the argument was avoided, and her true interest was uncovered.

2. Observations & Feelings

It can feel awkward to give a friend feedback when that person is behaving in a way you find displeasing. Additionally, if the situation is emotionally charged, the conversation can be even more difficult. You may be clumsy in what you try to convey, say things that you don't mean, and potentially resort to labeling or name calling. The conversation can easily escalate to an unproductive situation.

For friendships to be healthy and sustainable, it's important to share your observations and feelings. If your friend was unhappy with something *you* are doing, wouldn't you want to know about it so that you could change your behavior, especially if you were doing it inadvertently? The key is to be as thoughtful and objective as possible so that the conversation can stay focused on recovery.

Even with a friend, it's important to prepare for feedback conversations. Ask yourself:

- If I were an outside observer and didn't know either person, how would I describe the behavior that I see? What are my unbiased observations of the situation?

- How do I feel when my friend behaves in this way?
- What am I contributing to the situation? Are my actions and feelings appropriate for the situation? Do I need to adjust or take responsibility for any of my own actions or reactions?
- What is the desired behavior I would like to see in the future?

A client, John, once called me to vent and lament about a friend, Dan, who happened to also be a teammate at work. Dan was having marital issues, and, not surprisingly, bringing a lot of negative emotions to work. For the past month, he had been short-tempered with everyone on the team and only focused on the negatives during team meetings.

Dan was the team's expert in a particular area of the business and was usually very generous in assisting others when they had questions. More recently, however, he always had his door closed, which scared teammates away, and when they were able to catch him for a question, Dan was incredibly condescending.

Unaware of his personal situation, the team started talking quite negatively about Dan, and John was finding it increasingly difficult to refrain from getting caught up in the drama. He knew he needed to talk to Dan and so he asked for my help.

John shared Dan's behavior with me:

> "I know I need to talk with him, but we've never had this kind of conversation before. We've always been great friends, but the way he's acting is aggravating to me and the team. Can't I just tell him to stop being an SOB?"

> "Well, certainly you can," I said, "but could he get defensive at your use of SOB?"

> "He's so wound up with his marital situation, he proba-

bly would. Plus, he doesn't want anyone at work to know what's going on in his personal life," John said.

"And if you tell him to stop acting like an SOB, would he know what behavior to change? Does he have the same definition of the term as you do?" I asked.

"No," chuckled John, "using the label wouldn't describe the behavior that I think needs to be different. I guess I need to think through this a little more."

John and I continued to talk through the situation, focusing on his observations and feelings in response to the preparation questions. He decided that he would invite John for a coffee later that day to have the conversation.

John reached out the next day to tell me how it went. He recounted that at first it was awkward. Dan could sense that he was uncomfortable about something.

"What's up?" Dan asked.

"Well, I have something that I need to share with you. It's kind of awkward because we have never had this kind of conversation before, but because we're such good friends, I feel that I need to be candid with you," John said.

"Okay," Dan said, waiting for John to go on.

"Well, I know that you have had a lot going on at home, and it seems that the stress from that situation is overflowing into the workplace and having an effect on the team, myself included," John said. "When we're in meetings, you seem to only point out why people's ideas won't work but yet you don't offer any other ideas yourself."

"Mm-hmm," expressed Dan.

"You seem to always have your door closed now when it used to be open. We really appreciate your advice, but now you answer our questions in one or two clipped sentences, when you used to give much longer, more helpful explanations. We feel that you don't have time for us anymore," John said.

"Yeah, I can see that. It's just been a really tough time. I haven't had much energy left for work," Dan said.

"I know you're going through a lot right now and don't want anyone at work to know. I just felt you should know how people are feeling so that it doesn't have any negative repercussions for you and the team." John shared.

"I really appreciate the heads up and your candor," Dan said. "I guess I didn't realize how much I was wearing my emotions on my sleeve at work, and I certainly don't want to take it out on you or the team. I'll try to manage my negativity and look for ways to be more helpful to everyone."

I congratulated John on managing the conversation well and for sharing his observations and feelings in a constructive manner. He was pleased and hopeful with the outcome of his conversation with Dan. Discussing his concerns in this way allowed him to identify the offending behavior and accompanying emotions while still focusing on the relationship and recovery.

While disagreements with friends is never fun, try focusing on interests, rather than positions, and constructively share your observations and feelings so you can get past it and enjoy the benefits of the relationship.

Ending a Relationship

You don't typically hear about "breakups" when it comes to friendships, like you do in romantic relationships. My question is, "Why not?" As we have explored, and you already know, not all friendships are a good fit or sometimes they run their course. Yet we often just let them fade away or worse, we "ghost" them—cut off all communication and disappear. (I am not a fan of "ghosting." It seems cruel.)

Wouldn't it be more kind and loving to provide closure when a relationship has run its course or is not a good fit? I have had a couple of relationships fade away that I have wondered about. Did I do something? If I had known that the person didn't like something, could I have adjusted my behavior to keep the relationship going? I will never know.

Candidly, I have only had one of these conversations in my life. I leveraged the Observations & Feelings technique to open the conversation about what wasn't working for me in the relationship. We both stayed calm, and she gave me feedback as well. Not surprisingly, the relationship wasn't working for her either. While uncomfortable, I'm glad it happened this way. It gave us both closure, and I learned something from the relationship, as well from as the conversation itself.

You need to decide for yourself how to best handle relationships that don't work for you. In the spirit of working to keep joy in our lives, I encourage all of us to handle these sensitive situations with courage and kindness.

Whether friendships last a lifetime or only a few months, they are an important part of a Joychiever's life. So come to port in Relationships Harbor and find the right friends to share your voyage.

Endnotes

i   Mejia, Zameena. "Harvard's Longest Study of Adult Life Reveals How You Can Be Happier and More Successful." CNBC, March 20, 2018. Accessed May 28, 2020. https://www.cnbc.com/2018/03/20/this-harvard-study-reveals-how-you-can-be-happier-and-more-successful.html.

"ME" MOMENTS MARKET: QUIT GIVING AND TAKE A LITTLE

"You have to create little pockets of joy in your life to take care of yourself."

— *Jonathan Van Ness*

I love an open-air food market. I have visited many different markets in a variety of countries, and I am always fascinated with the interesting foods, delectable smells, and intriguing sights I find there. I particularly love spice markets. They are visually beautiful, with overflowing baskets of bright red, yellow, green, and orange spices. I love to smell the sweet cinnamon and imagine tasting the spicy ground chili pepper and relaxing with the lovely lavender.

Can you visualize yourself there?

Now I want you to visualize these baskets overflowing with "ME" moments—ways that you could spend time focusing solely on you. If you could "shop" at this "ME" Moments Market weekly, what would you choose? What are the ways that you would enjoy spending five minutes, 15 minutes, 60 minutes, or more? Would you "buy" a quick nap? Maybe a five-minute meditation? How about a walk around the block? Or how about choosing three minutes to simply sit still, breathe, and do nothing?

"ME" moments are brief vacations from all the commitments in your life. The harder you push, the more you need to replenish yourself. It's critical that you fill, and refill, the YOU reservoir on a regular basis by spending quality time with *yourself*. Spending this time can:

- Improve your mood
- Decrease irritability
- Increase patience
- Lessen resentment
- Boost concentration
- Elevate productivity
- Enhance creativity and problem-solving ability

The key is to engage in an activity that brings you joy or relaxation, even if the moments are brief. Don't worry about accomplishing something or learning something. This is the time to relax and replenish yourself.

How Do You Find the Time?

With an overachiever's overscheduled life, it can be challenging to find space for yourself. Like all other aspects of joy, finding time to unwind also has be intentional. Be on the lookout for stolen minutes or ways to incorporate "ME" moments into activities in which you already engage.

For example, my husband was trying to survive a particularly stressful and busy time with work. One morning, I tried to encourage him to go for a run or meditate when he said, "I don't have time for any of that. I barely have time to drink my coffee."

I said, "Well, then, take these five minutes to really enjoy your coffee. Put the phone away and really *taste* the coffee. Smell it. Remember the time when we bought that coffee on our trip to Brazil." In that way, rather than simply mainlining the caffeine, he could transform his morning coffee into a "ME" moment.

To incorporate other "ME" moments into your day, you could spend a few extra minutes in the shower in the morning just to breathe or let your mind wander. During your commute, you could listen to an audio book or your favorite music.

On a pretty day, you could eat your lunch outside or leave the office a couple of minutes early for an external meeting to take in some daylight. After you accomplish a task, try to take a few minutes to stand up and stretch. If you fly frequently for work, instead of answering emails during your flight, choose to read a book or watch a movie instead.

When at home, take a nap or pamper yourself while the kids are napping. While walking the dog, listen to an active meditation or your affirmations.

With a little bit of thought, you can find many ways to work small "ME" moments into your existing routine.

A Morning Ritual

One way to focus on yourself is to establish a morning ritual. A morning ritual enables you to center yourself and nourish your mind, body, and spirit. The ritual itself can be as simple or as involved as you choose to make it and can include activities such as exercise, meditation, reading, or spending time with your family.

Your morning ritual:

- **Helps you to set the tone for the day**
  In many ways, waking up in the morning can feel like a

clean slate. You get to choose what mood you want to be in for the day. By focusing on positive practices first thing in the morning, you can stack your day for optimism.

- **Positions you for productivity**
  Many people use a clear mind in the morning to lay out what they want to get done in the day. With minimal clutter already in your head, you can focus on what is most important for a productive day.

- **Enables better stress management**
  The temptation to reach for your mobile device to check email, news, and social media when you first wake up is high. However, if you can refrain from filling your brain with work pressures and negativity from the world, you can keep cortisol and adrenaline at bay for a few extra minutes or hours.

- **Provides time for creativity**
  When your mind has a chance to wander freely or play, creativity can flourish. By giving your mind some space in the morning, you may come up with great new ideas. After all, many people claim that they come up with their best ideas during their morning shower.

- **Gives you a reason to get out of bed**
  A morning ritual can give you something pleasurable to look forward to so that you won't want to hit the snooze button repeatedly. Once you find the right mix of activity or calmness that gets your day off to a perfect start, you'll never want to miss out on your ritual.

- **Is entirely about you**
  You may have to set your alarm a little earlier, but a morning ritual is all for you. No one is expecting anything of you during this time. It's your time to keep the entire world at bay whether it's for 15 minutes, an hour, or several hours.

Many successful people have morning rituals.[i] Barack Obama, former US President, starts every day with cardio and a strength workout and then has breakfast with his family. Jack Dorsey, founder of Twitter, meditates and runs six miles every day. Media mogul, Oprah Winfrey, wakes up to 20 minutes of meditation, followed by a 15-minute workout. Howard Schultz, CEO of Starbucks, not surprisingly, focuses on coffee. He walks his dogs and works out every morning and then makes coffee for himself and his wife.

Overcoming the Guilt

Taking time for yourself can feel selfish, and many people feel guilty just thinking about it. There's a list of housework that needs to be done, kids who need caring for, or work that's demanding your attention. You can easily fall into a never-ending guilt trap if you can't accept the absolute need to care for yourself, just like you do for others.

Although you may feel like you can't take the time, here is something you may want to consider: **Other people benefit from your "ME" time too.** Your family, work colleagues, and friends will experience a happier, recharged, and refreshed you, rather than an overwhelmed, irritable, short-tempered you. By taking care of yourself, you also take care of them.

Having the Conversation

An important piece of this puzzle is how you express your need for "ME" time and your willingness to support others to have theirs. If you simply say, "I need time for myself," your partner might offer a sarcasm-laden response of, "Yeah, so do I." It may start the conversation off on the wrong note.

It's important to clearly express your needs and invite others in your family to participate in "ME" time, as well. As a team, on a weekly basis, discuss when you can find or schedule your moments. You may want a few hours on Saturday morning, while your partner may need some time on Thursday night. In the same way that you plan for all the other activities in your life, make sure to include some "ME" time in your week. The key is not to get too stressed out and make this yet another thing to schedule. Keep it simple.

One way to free up your family schedule is to think of activities that could be consolidated, eliminated, delegated, or outsourced so that there is more space available for "ME" time. You don't have to come up with hours every week. Start small and see what happens.

Ideas for "ME" Time

If you're struggling with what to do with your "ME" time, here are some ideas:

If you have 5-10 minutes

- Stretch
- Breathe
- Do nothing
- Listen to music
- Read a favorite poem
- Listen to affirmations
- Watch the clouds go by
- Walk stairs
- Snuggle your pet
- Dream about your next vacation

If you have 15-30 minutes

- Read a book

- Do a crossword puzzle or Sudoku
- Trim flowers from your garden
- Go for a walk
- Take the dog to a nearby park
- Take a bath
- Enjoy a facial mask
- Buy a gift for yourself online

If you have 30-60 minutes

- Get a massage
- Take a nap
- Meditate
- Schedule a class that you've always wanted to take just for fun
- Go for a bike ride
- Visit a botanical garden or do some gardening of your own
- Engage in one of your favorite hobbies

When overachievers have a spare few minutes, they will often go to their mobile devices to check email, the news or social media. Joychievers, on the other hand, work to manage that temptation and instead take the time for something joyful. To discover what activities work best for you, simply try a few.

- If you've never meditated before, try a simple three-minute "refresh" using an app on your phone. There are many to choose from. Calm, Headspace, and Insight Timer are a few.

- Water can be extremely soothing. A brief soak in the tub or a quick shower can refresh and exhilarate. Try experimenting with scents such as soothing lavender or invigorating peppermint.

- Give yourself a quick spa treatment. A facial mask, for both women and men, can bring great pleasure and is terrific for the skin.

- A simple yoga stretch can work wonders for the body and soul. Try a tree pose or downward dog and simply breathe for a few minutes to clear your head.

- A book by your side can be one of your best "ME" friends. Reading, even for a few minutes, can lift you outside of your routine and take you to another place and time.

- Listening to music can give you an energy boost or calm your mind. Have your music accessible so that you can quickly choose the music to fit your mood.

- Give yourself a mini hand massage. Hold your left hand up, palm facing outward. Using your right hand, pull the fingers back toward your wrist until you feel a stretch. Repeat the stretch on your right hand. Then massage the inside and outside of each hand and gently shake them out.

Stop by the "ME" Moments Market each week to select what you need for the upcoming seven days. Prioritize the focus on *yourself* as high as everything else in your life so that you are continuously replenished and recharged.

You'll find the more you "shop" at the "ME" Moments Market, the more joy you'll find in your life.

Endnotes

i   "The Morning Routines of the Rich and Famous." *Glamour*. April 12, 2018. Accessed May 26, 2020. https://www.glamourmagazine.co.uk/gallery/morning-routines-of-successful-people.

THE JOYCHIEVER CREDO: ACTIONS FOR LIFELONG HAPPINESS

"One day or day one, you decide."

— *Unknown*

While you may have come to the end of the book, your journey is still ahead of you. I'm hopeful that you can see it's possible to be a high achiever AND have joy. The goal is to spend as much time as possible in your "Happy Place." Let the Joychiever Credo guide your way.

Joychiever Credo

- **Seek joy as a passionate journey**
  You literally only live once so why not enjoy the ride? Living with joy as a regular mandate, rather than only something you allow yourself after you accomplish everything on your achievement list, will enrich and fulfill your life in ways you never knew were possible. Time is ticking so go after it! Seek joy!

- **Encourage others to seek joy**
  As you experience your joy, can you pay it forward? In what

ways can you help others find their joy? There are any number of ways to help people along their journeys. Be proactive with your encouragement.

- **Refuse to live by chance and postpone joy until after success**
  Live your life on purpose for joy, rather than expecting it to just happen. Doggedly pursue happiness as much as you chase after the next rung on the career ladder. Be unapologetic about putting joy at the top of your priority list. As Eleanor Roosevelt said, "Life is what you make of it."

- **View the world with positivity**
  Engage the world in ways to rewire your brain towards a positivity bias, rather than a negativity bias. Focus on the 40 bits of information your brain processes every second that help your glass to be full, rather than empty.

- **Have a clear set of values that guide your decisions**
  Your values make up the undercurrent that drives your life. So many people have never identified their top priorities or if they have, they put them aside. Consider your values regularly to ensure your choices are aligned with what is most important to you. They are your inner spring for joy.

- **Play to your strengths in specific contexts**
  You spend one-third of your life at work. Engage the seven steps discussed in Chapter Five to find clarity about your True Self strengths and associated contexts so that you can lean into your strengths as often as possible in both your work and home life.

- **Engage in leisure or hobbies to complement your work life**
  Everyone needs more fun. In a highly scheduled life, it's critical to find an escape from all of its demands. Find some time for yourself or ask your family and friends to have fun with

you. As the old proverb says, "All work and no play makes Jack a dull boy."

- **Make physical health a critical priority**
  Stress is a silent killer. You know it. I know it. Yet we keep ignoring our bodies when they show us the warning signs. Without your health, you have nothing. Prioritizing your sleep and making time for exercise are two of the best things you can do for your body.

- **Deliberately nurture joy-inducing relationships in all areas of your life**
  Relationships are one of the biggest factors that influence longevity. Consider the components of great romantic relationships as ways to also nurture your friendships. Look for those friends who regularly make you smile.

- **Take moments for yourself on a frequent basis**
  Find your ME moments. It's okay to take the time for you, and only you. Ideally, take a few minutes every day or at a minimum, seek a few moments a week.

The Joychiever Credo can feel overwhelming if you have never thought about these areas before. In order to focus on what you need to do right now, try the following Stop-Start-Continue Model to help you set your specific action steps for your journey.

Stop-Start-Continue Model

You may have heard of the Stop-Start-Continue model before and even used it, whether for a project at work or in personal reflection. It's an incredibly effective model to help you to start to move toward your joy goals. Take out a piece of paper and create three columns: Stop, Start, and Continue.

Stop

I want you to envision yourself in one year from now. Imagine that you have failed in accomplishing your goals and are no more joyful than you are now. What might be some of the reasons that you didn't get there? What are the behaviors, activities, mindsets, or bad habits that got in your way? Are there things that you need to put on your Stop list so they don't impede your progress? Write them down.

Start

What new behaviors, activities, or mindsets do you want to start working on now or incorporate into your regular routine? You don't have to start working on all of these items on Day 1 but create a list for the new habits that you want to develop.

Continue

No doubt you're already doing some great things for yourself when it comes to self-happiness. What are the behaviors, activities, and mindsets that you want to continue? Additionally, for any of those activities, can you take them up a notch? If you exercise twice a week, can you make it three times? Can you express gratitude more often in a day? Can you volunteer for more projects at work that leverage your strengths?

Know that there is so much joy within you just waiting to be released. Once you have your three lists, it's time to get moving.

"It is good to have an end to journey toward, but it is the journey that matters in the end."

—Ursula Le Guin

EPILOGUE

As I write this epilogue, it has been almost four years to the day that I left my "Lauren" life. That moment began my joy journey, but it wasn't until a year ago that I started my Joychiever Journey. It was then that I became clear that being an achiever and having joy could co-exist and even co-thrive.

My new business venture is doing very well, and I feel like I have more control over my life. I still travel but not nearly at the same hectic pace as before. I only have the highest status on one airline, rather than two, and I am surviving quite fine. I have been able to set some boundaries around my work schedule, and the weekends are for family, friends, fun, and leisure.

I only experience one or two signs of stress now, and they are usually very short term. I have a few newer friends who have been an excellent source of support, encouragement, and fun. I am aligned with my True Self and consistently feel like I'm in my Happy Place.

Over the four years, I've had numerous conversations with over-achievers who want to live differently. Some have been stuck in a rut and don't know how to get out. Others have had the courage to stand up for their needs and are now searching for a different path forward. It's clear that all of them have been in search of more joy and want to believe it's possible.

What's even more poignant is that I am writing this book during a monumental world crisis—the COVID-19 pandemic. Talk about the world needing some joy. So many of us have struggled financially and emotionally during this time.

Yet during these challenging times, I have seen numerous people continuously reaching for joy. Neighbors singing to one another from their balconies. Drive-by birthday parties. People working from home and now spending their regular commuting time with their families or focusing on themselves. Everyone now knows the concept of a Zoom Happy Hour, and so much gratitude has been expressed for healthcare workers, package delivery personnel, and countless others who have helped us keep living our lives. It has been amazing!

While there is still so much uncertainty ahead for us, my hope is that the overachievers of the world can leverage what they have learned about themselves during this time to become Joychievers. My fear, however, is that once offices open up again and the world goes back to "normal," overachievers will put these lessons aside and go back to nonstop activity filled with stress, anxiety, and worry.

If you've read to this point, then you are ready to be different. If you have friends intent on returning to the whirlwind, please gift them a copy of this book, for their sakes.

APPENDIX

Values List

Abundance	Acceptance	Accomplishment
Accountability	Achievement	Advancement
Adventure	Advocacy	Altruism
Ambition	Appreciation	Authority
Autonomy	Balance	Boldness
Brilliance	Challenge	Charity
Collaboration	Commitment	Community
Compassion	Competence	Confidence
Consistency	Contribution	Control
Creativity	Credibility	Curiosity
Decisiveness	Dependability	Discipline
Diversity	Education	Empathy
Enthusiasm	Ethics	Excellence
Expertise	Fairness	Family
Fitness	Freedom	Friendship
Fun	Generosity	Grace
Growth	Happiness	Health

Honesty	Humility	Humor
Inclusiveness	Independence	Individuality
Innovation	Inspiration	Integrity
Intelligence	Intuition	Joy
Justice	Kindness	Knowledge
Leadership	Learning	Logic
Love	Loyalty	Mercy
Motivation	Obedience	Open-Mindedness
Optimism	Originality	Passion
Patience	Peace	Perfection
Persuasion	Philanthropy	Power
Preparedness	Proactivity	Productivity
Professionalism	Punctuality	Purpose
Quality	Reason	Recognition
Relationship	Reliability	Reputation
Resilience	Resourcefulness	Respect
Responsibility	Responsiveness	Risk-Taking
Self-Control	Self-Discipline	Service
Spirituality	Stability	Stewardship
Success	Teamwork	Tolerance
Trustworthiness	Understanding	Uniqueness
Versatility	Vision	Wealth
Well-Being	Wisdom	Zeal

Values Definitions[i]

Abundance: 1: an ample quantity; profusion **2:** affluence, wealth **3:** relative degree of plentifulness	**Acceptance: 1:** the act of accepting something or someone **2:** the fact of being accepted. **3:** approval	**Accomplishment: 1:** to bring about (a result) by effort **2:** to bring to completion; fulfill. **3:** to succeed in reaching (a stage in a progression)
Accountability: 1: an obligation or willingness to accept responsibility or to account for one's actions	**Achievement: 1:** a result gained by effort **2:** to carry out successfully **3:** to get or attain as the result of exertion	**Advancement: 1:** progression to a higher stage of development **2:** to bring or move forward **3:** to raise to a higher rank **4:** improvement
Adventure: 1: an undertaking usually involving danger and unknown risks **2:** the encountering of risks **3:** an exciting or remarkable experience	**Advocacy: 1:** the act or process of supporting a cause or proposal **2:** to support or argue for (a cause, policy, etc.) **3:** to plead in favor of	**Altruism:** unselfish regard for or devotion to the welfare of others
Ambition: 1: an ardent desire for rank, fame or power **2:** desire to achieve a particular end	**Appreciation: 1:** a feeling or expression of admiration, approval or gratitude **2:** judgment or evaluation, especially, a favorable critical estimate **3:** sensitive awareness	**Authority: 1:** power to influence or command thought, opinion or behavior **2:** freedom granted by one in authority

i   Adapted from the Merriam-Webster Dictionary

Autonomy: 1: the quality or state of being self-governing, especially the right of self-government **2:** self-directing freedom and especially moral independence	**Balance: 1:** physical equilibrium **2:** the ability to retain one's balance **3:** mental and emotional steadiness	**Boldness: 1:** showing or requiring a fearless daring spirit **2:** adventurous, free **3:** standing out prominently
Brilliance: 1: distinguished by unusual mental keenness or alertness **2:** striking, distinctive, excellent	**Challenge: 1:** a stimulating task or problem **2:** a calling to account or into question; protest	**Charity: 1:** generosity and helpfulness especially toward the needy or suffering **2:** benevolent goodwill toward or love of humanity
Collaboration: to work jointly with others or together especially in an intellectual endeavor	**Commitment: 1:** to obligate or pledge oneself **2:** an agreement or pledge to do something in the future	**Community: 1:** a unified body of individuals **2:** a group of people with a common characteristic or interest living together within a larger society
Compassion: sympathetic consciousness of others' distress together with a desire to alleviate it	**Competence:** the quality or state of having sufficient knowledge, judgment, skill or strength	**Community: 1:** a unified body of individuals **2:** a group of people with a common characteristic or interest living together within a larger society

Compassion: sympathetic consciousness of others' distress together with a desire to alleviate it	**Competence:** the quality or state of having sufficient knowledge, judgment, skill or strength	**Confidence: 1:** faith or belief that one will act in a right, proper or effective way **2:** a feeling or consciousness of one's powers or of reliance on one's circumstances
Consistency: 1: agreement or harmony of parts or features to one another or a whole **2:** harmony of conduct or practice	**Contribution: 1:** to give or supply in common with others **2:** to play a significant part in bringing about an end or result	**Control: 1:** to exercise restraining or directing influence over; regulate **2:** to have power over
Creativity: 1: to make or bring into existence something new **2:** marked by the ability or power to create	**Credibility: 1:** the quality or power of inspiring belief **2:** offering reasonable grounds for being believed	**Curiosity: 1:** desire to know **2:** marked by desire to investigate and learn
Decisiveness: 1: to make a final choice or judgment about **2:** resolute, determined	**Dependability: 1:** capable of being trusted or depended on **2:** reliable or trustworthy	**Discipline: 1:** control gained by enforcing obedience or order **2:** orderly or prescribed conduct or pattern of behavior **3:** self-control

Diversity: 1: the inclusion of different types of people (such as people of different races or cultures) in a group or organization **2:** an instance of being composed of differing elements or qualities	**Education: 1:** the action or process of educating or of being educated **2:** the knowledge and development resulting from the process of being educated **3:** having an education **4:** giving evidence of training or practice; skilled	**Empathy:** the action of understanding, being aware of and being sensitive to others' feelings, thoughts and experiences
Enthusiasm: 1: strong excitement of feeling **2:** inspiring zeal or fervor	**Ethics: 1:** the discipline dealing with what is good and bad and with moral duty and obligation **2:** a set of moral principles	**Excellence:** very good of its kind; superior
Expertise: 1: the skill of an expert **2:** having, involving or displaying special skill or knowledge derived from training or experience	**Fairness: 1:** fair or impartial treatment **2:** lack of favoritism toward one side or another	**Excellence:** very good of its kind; superior
Expertise: 1: the skill of an expert **2:** having, involving or displaying special skill or knowledge derived from training or experience	**Fairness: 1:** fair or impartial treatment **2:** lack of favoritism toward one side or another	**Family: 1:** the basic unit in society **2:** a group of individuals living under one roof and usually under one head **3:** a group of things related by common characteristics

Fitness: 1: the quality or state of being fit **2:** sound, physically and mentally	**Freedom: 1:** the quality or state of being free **2:** the absence of necessity, coercion or constraint in choice or action **3:** unrestricted **4:** the quality of being frank, open or outspoken **5:** a political right	**Friendship: 1:** one attached to another by affection or esteem **2:** the state of being friends
Fun: 1: what provides amusement or enjoyment **2:** a mood for finding or making amusement **3:** to indulge in banter or play	**Generosity: 1:** liberal in giving **2:** a generous act	**Grace:** disposition to or an act or instance of kindness, courtesy or clemency
Growth: 1: to spring up and develop to maturity **2:** to promote the development of	**Happiness: 1:** a state of well-being and contentment; joy **2:** a pleasurable or satisfying experience	**Health: 1:** the condition of being sound in body, mind or spirit **2:** the general condition of the body
Honesty: 1: adherence to the facts; sincerity **2:** fairness and straightforwardness of conduct	**Humility: 1:** freedom from pride or arrogance **2:** not proud or haughty; not arrogant or assertive	**Humor:** that quality which appeals to a sense of the funny or amusing

Inclusiveness: 1: including everyone 2: broad in orientation or scope	Independence: 1: not subject to control by others 2: not requiring or relying on something else 3: not contingent	Individuality: 1: total character peculiar to and distinguishing an individual from others 2: separate or distinct existence 3: a particular being or thing as distinguished from a class, species or collection
Innovation: 1: a new idea, method or device; novelty 2: the introduction of something new	Inspiration: 1: the action or power of moving the intellect or emotions 2: the act of influencing or suggesting opinions 3: having an animating or exalting effect 4: outstanding or brilliant in a way or to a degree suggestive of divine	Integrity: 1: firm adherence to a code of especially moral or artistic values 2: an unimpaired condition; soundness 3: the quality or state of being complete or undivided
Intelligence: 1: having or indicating a high or satisfactory degree of intellect and mental capacity 2: revealing or reflecting good judgment or sound thought 3: mental acuteness	Intuition: 1: the power or faculty of attaining to direct knowledge or cognition without evident rational thought and inference 2: immediate apprehension or cognition 3: quick and ready insight	Joy: 1: the emotion evoked by well-being, success or good fortune; delight 2: the expression or exhibition of such emotion; gaiety 3: a state of happiness or felicity

Justice: 1:the maintenance or administration of what is just, especially by the impartial adjustment of conflicting claims or the assignment of merited rewards or punishments **2:** having a basis in or conforming to fact or reason; reasonable **3:** conforming to a standard of correctness	**Kindness:** of a sympathetic or helpful nature	**Knowledge: 1:** the fact or condition of being aware of something **2:** the range of one's information or understanding
Leadership: providing direction or guidance	**Learning: 1:** to gain knowledge or understanding of or skill in by study, instruction or experience **2:** to come to be able	**Logic:** capable of reasoning or of using reason in an orderly, cogent fashion
Love: 1: warm attachment, enthusiasm or devotion **2:** unselfish, loyal and benevolent **3:** concern for the good of another	**Loyalty:** unswerving in allegiance	**Mercy:** compassion or forbearance shown especially to an offender or to one subject to one's power
Motivation: 1: to urge or drive forward or on **2:** to impart motion to	**Obedience: 1:** submissive to the restraint or command of authority **2:** willing to obey	**Open-Mindedness:** receptive to arguments or ideas

Optimism 1: a doctrine that this world is the best possible world 2: an inclination to put the most favorable construction upon actions and events or to anticipate the best possible outcome	Originality: 1: freshness of aspect, design or style 2: the power of independent thought or constructive imagination	Passion: 1: intense, driving or overmastering feeling or conviction 2: enthusiastic; ardent
Patience: 1: bearing pains or trials calmly or without complaint 2: not hasty or impetuous 3: steadfast despite opposition, difficulty or adversity	Peace: 1: a state of tranquility or quiet: 2: freedom from disquieting or oppressive thoughts or emotions 3: harmony in personal relations	Perfection: 1: freedom from fault or defect 2: an exemplification of supreme excellence 3: an unsurpassable degree of accuracy or excellence
Persuasion: 1: to move by argument, entreaty or expostulation to a belief, position or course of action 2: to plead with	Philanthropy: 1: goodwill to fellow members of the human race, especially to promote human welfare 2: an act or gift done or made for humanitarian purpose	Power: 1: possession of control, authority or influence over others 2: ability to act or produce an effect 3: legal or official authority, capacity or right

Preparedness: the action or process of making something ready for use or service or of getting ready for some occasion, test or duty	**Proactivity:** acting in anticipation of future problems, needs or changes	**Productivity:** **1:** having the quality or power of producing, especially in abundance **2:** effective in bringing about **3:** yielding results, benefits or profits
Professionalism: **1:** characterized by or conforming to the technical or ethical standards of a profession **2:** exhibiting a courteous, conscientious and generally businesslike manner in the workplace	**Punctuality: 1:** being on time **2:** prompt	**Purpose: 1:** something set up as an object or end to be attained **2:** intentionally; resolute; determined **3:** setting goals
Quality: 1: degree of excellence **2:** superiority in kind	**Reason: 1:** a sufficient ground of explanation or of logical defense, especially something (such as a principle or law) that supports a conclusion or explains a fact **2:** the power of comprehending, inferring or thinking especially in orderly, rational ways	**Recognition: 1:** to acknowledge formally as being of a particular status **2:** special notice or attention

Relationship: 1: the relation connecting or binding participants in a relationship 2: a state of affairs existing between those having relations or dealings	Reliability: 1: suitable or fit to be relied on; dependable 2: to have confidence based on experience	Reputation: 1: overall quality or character as seen or judged by people in general 2: recognition by other people of some characteristic or ability 3: a place in public esteem or regard 4: good name
Resilience: an ability to recover from or adjust easily to misfortune or change	Resourcefulness: 1: able to meet situations 2: capable of devising ways and means	Reputation: 1: overall quality or character as seen or judged by people in general 2: recognition by other people of some characteristic or ability 3: a place in public esteem or regard 4: good name
Resilience: an ability to recover from or adjust easily to misfortune or change	Resourcefulness: 1: able to meet situations 2: capable of devising ways and means	Respect: 1: high or special regard 2: esteemed
Responsibility: 1: moral, legal or mental accountability 2: able to answer for one's conduct and obligations 3: reliability; trustworthiness	Responsiveness: 1: quick to respond or react appropriately 2: to say something in return 3: make an answer	Risk-Taking: the act or fact of doing something that involves danger or risk in order to achieve a goal

Self-Control: restraint exercised over one's own impulses, emotions or desires	**Self-Discipline:** correction or regulation of oneself for the sake of improvement	**Service: 1:** to answer the needs of **2:** to be of use 3: contribution to the welfare of others
Spirituality: 1: of, relating to, consisting of or affecting the spirit; incorporeal **2:** of or relating to sacred matters **3:** concerned with religious values	**Stability: 1:** firmly established; steadfast **2:** not changing or fluctuating **3:** unvarying; enduring 4: steady in purpose	**Stewardship:** the conducting, supervising or managing of something
Success: 1: to turn out well **2:** to attain a desired object or end **3:** favorable or desired outcome	**Teamwork:** work done by several associates with each doing a part but all subordinating personal prominence to the efficiency of the whole	**Tolerance: 1:** sympathy or indulgence for beliefs or practices differing from or conflicting with one's own **2:** the act of allowing something **3:** the allowable deviation from a standard
Trustworthiness: worthy of confidence	**Understanding: 1:** a mental grasp, comprehension **2:** tolerant, sympathetic	**Uniqueness: 1:** being the only one **2:** being without a like or equal

Versatility: 1: embracing a variety of subjects, fields or skills **2:** turning with ease from one thing to another **3:** changing or fluctuating readily	**Vision: 1:** the act or power of seeing **2:** the act or power of imagination	**Wealth:** abundance of valuable material possessions or resources
Well-Being: the state of being happy, healthy or prosperous	**Wisdom: 1:** ability to discern inner qualities and relationships; insight **2:** good sense; judgment	**Zeal: 1:** eagerness and ardent interest in pursuit of something **2:** fervor

BIBLIOGRAPHY

Achor, Shawn. *Before Happiness: The 5 Hidden Keys to Achieving Success, Spreading Happiness, and Sustaining Positive Change.* New York: Crown Business, 2013.

Achor, Shawn. *The Happiness Advantage: How a Positive Brain Fuels Success in Work and Life.* New York: Currency, 2018.

Ackerman, Courtney. "Learned Helplessness: Seligman's Theory of Depression (+ Cure)." PositivePsychology.com. May 12, 2020. Accessed March 03, 2020. https://positivepsychology.com/learned-helplessness-seligman-theory-depression-cure/.

Agrawal, Sangeeta and Ben Wigert. "Employee Burnout, Part 1: The 5 Main Causes." Gallup.com. May 14, 2020. Accessed July 03, 2020. https://www.gallup.com/workplace/237059/employee-burnout-part-main-causes.aspx.

Berkovic, Eva. "Why Does Your Brain Love Negativity? The Negativity Bias." Marbella International University Centre. February 9, 2017. Accessed April 22, 2020. https://www.miuc.org/brain-love-negativity-negativity-bias/.

Bstan-'dzin-rgya-mtsho and Howard C. Cutler. *The Art of Happiness: 10th Anniversary Gift Edition.* Sydney, N.S.W.: Hachette Australia, 2009.

Buckingham, Marcus. *Go Put Your Strengths to Work: 6 Powerful Steps to Achieve Outstanding Performance*. New York: Free Press, 2011.

Cherry, Kendra. "What Is the Negativity Bias?" Verywell Mind. April 29, 2020. Accessed April 29, 2020. https://www.verywellmind.com/negative-bias-4589618.

Clave-Brule, M., A. Mazloum, R. J. Park, E. J. Harbottle and C. L. Birmingham. "Managing anxiety in eating disorders with knitting." Accessed May 01, 2020. https://pubmed.ncbi.nlm.nih.gov/19367130/.

Collective Evolution. "The Top 5 Regrets Of The Dying." *HuffPost*. August 03, 2013. Accessed March 02, 2020. https://www.huffpost.com/entry/top-5-regrets-of-the-dying_n_3640593.

Conlon, Ciara. "40 Simple Ways to Practice Gratitude." Lifehack. July 08, 2019. Accessed April 19, 2020. https://www.lifehack.org/articles/communication/40-simple-ways-practice-gratitude.html.

Dartmouth College. "Kindness Health Facts." Accessed 06 August 2020. https://www.dartmouth.edu/wellness/emotional/rakhealthfacts.pdf.

Dockrill, Peter. "There's a Strange Explosion of Certain Meditative Practices in America Right Now." ScienceAlert. November 12, 2018. Accessed July 03, 2020. https://www.sciencealert.com/yoga-and-meditation-in-the-us-are-totally-exploding-right-now.

"The Effects of Stress on Your Body." WebMD. December 10, 2017. Accessed May 08, 2020. https://www.webmd.com/balance/stress-management/effects-of-stress-on-your-body.

Emling, Shelley. "Here's Yet Another Important Reason to Get

Enough Shut-Eye." *HuffPost*. July 24, 2013. Accessed May 11, 2020. https://www.huffpost.com/entry/sleep-depriva-tion-effects-aging-skin_n_3644269.

Fredrickson, Barbara. *Positivity*. New York: Harmony Books, 2009.

Friedman, Lauren F. and Kevin Loria. "11 Scientific Reasons You Should Be Spending More Time Outside." *Business Insider*. April 22, 2016. Accessed May 01, 2020. https://www.businessinsider.com/scientific-benefits-of-nature-out-doors-2016-4?r=US&IR=T.

Friedrich, Cathe. "5 Brain-Boosting Chemicals Released During Exercise." Cathe. March 24, 2019. Accessed April 19, 2020. https://cathe.com/5-brain-boosting-chemicals-re-leased-during-exercise/.

"The Morning Routines of the Rich and Famous." *Glamour*. April 12, 2018. Accessed May 26, 2020. https://www.glamourma-gazine.co.uk/gallery/morning-routines-of-successful-people.

Goleman, Daniel, and Richard J. Davidson. *Altered Traits: Science Reveals How Meditation Changes Your Mind, Brain, and Body*. New York: Avery, an Imprint of Penguin Random House LLC, 2018.

Golkar, Armita, Emilia Johansson, Maki Kasahara, Walter Osika, Aleksander Perski and Ivanka Savic. "The Influence of Work-Related Chronic Stress on the Regulation of Emo-tion and on Functional Connectivity in the Brain." *PLOS ONE*. (2014). 9(9). https://journals.plos.org/plosone/arti-cle?id=10.1371/journal.pone.0104550.

Hanson, Rick. *Hardwiring Happiness: The New Brain Science of Contentment, Calm, and Confidence*. New York: Harmony Books, 2016.

"Heart Health Improved by Sense of Purpose." March 10, 2015. Accessed July 24, 2020. https://www.medicalbrief.co.za/archives/heart-health-improved-by-sense-of-purpose/.

Health.gov. "Walk. Run. Dance. Play. What's Your Move?" Move Your Way. Accessed May 13, 2020. https://health.gov/moveyourway.

HHS Office, and President's Council on Sports, Fitness, and Nutrition. "Facts & Statistics." HHS.gov. January 26, 2017. Accessed May 13, 2020. https://www.hhs.gov/fitness/resource-center/facts-and-statistics/index.html.

HHS Office, and President's Council on Sports, Fitness, and Nutrition. "Physical Activity Guidelines for Americans." HHS.gov. February 01, 2019. Accessed April 22, 2020. https://www.hhs.gov/fitness/be-active/physical-activity-guidelines-for-americans/index.html.

Horsley, Kevin and Louis Fourie. *The Happy Mind: A Simple Guide to Living a Happier Life Starting Today.* Place of Publication Not Identified: Published by TCK Publishing, 2017.

"Is Social Connection a Path to Happiness? SimplyCircle Guest Post." SimplyCircle. September 04, 2018. Accessed May 01, 2020. https://simplycircle.com/social-connection-happiness/.

"Leisure Time." Psychology Wiki. Accessed April 29, 2020. https://psychology.wikia.org/wiki/Leisure_time.

MacMillan, Amanda. "7 Ways Daylight Saving Time Can Affect Your Health." Health.com. March 01, 2019. Accessed May 12, 2020. https://www.health.com/condition/sleep/daylight-saving-time-health-risks.

Mead, Elaine. "Personal Strengths & Weaknesses Defined (+ List of 92 Personal Strengths)." PositivePsychology.com. June 22,

2020. Accessed April 24, 2020. https://positivepsychology. com/what-are-your-strengths/.

Medina, John, and Tracy Cutchlow. *Brain Rules for Aging Well: 10 Principles for Staying Vital, Happy, and Sharp.* Seattle, WA: Pear Press, 2017.

Mejia, Zameena. "Harvard's Longest Study of Adult Life Reveals How You Can Be Happier and More Successful." CNBC. March 20, 2018. Accessed May 28, 2020. https://www.cnbc. com/2018/03/20/this-harvard-study-reveals-how-you-can-be-happier-and-more-successful.html.

"Sleep Deprivation Affects Face Appearance, Study Shows." *Huff-Post.* August 30, 2013. Accessed May 11, 2020. https://www. huffpost.com/entry/sleep-deprivation-face-appearance-ug-ly_n_3843913?guccounter=1&guce_referrer=aHR0cHM-6Ly9zZWFyY2gueWFob28uY29tLw&guce_referrer_sig=AQAAACQ9UxTsYZSIYuSx7SjQBHPx-xG-nUGVS7JKQTfZsA-uvAZhA76_lEAqb6uXB_f8irub-JAFeBU2NEi-ELfmv1-YmnIWWmTzDLXb0W-tD3IX-qO5weQX6tAKSGYE9W_02q3m3YEWUO4ag3AiR1Fp-fAFVw2HNmohkxloG48b3QdSd7iY.

National Institutes of Health. "Your Guide to Healthy Sleep." https://www.nhlbi.nih.gov/files/docs/public/sleep/healthy_sleep.pdf. Accessed July 23, 2020.

Oman, D., C. E. Thoresen and K. McMahon. "Volunteerism and Mortality Among the Community-dwelling Elderly." *Journal of Health Psychology.* (1999) *4*(3) 301–16. Accessed May 22, 2020. https://pubmed.ncbi.nlm.nih.gov/22021599/.

Petre, Alina. "13 Habits Linked to a Long Life (Backed by Science)." Healthline. April 8, 2019. Accessed March 02, 2020.

https://www.healthline.com/nutrition/13-habits-linked-to-a-long-life.

Robinson, Ken, and Lou Aronica. *Finding Your Element: Living a Life of Passion and Purpose.* New York: Viking, 2013.

Seligman, Martin E. P. *Flourish: A Visionary New Understanding of Happiness and Well-being.* New York: Atria, 2013.

Shea, Christopher. "A Brief History of Mindfulness in the USA and Its Impact on Our Lives." Psych Central. October 08, 2018. Accessed April 22, 2020. https://psychcentral.com/lib/a-brief-history-of-mindfulness-in-the-usa-and-its-impact-on-our-lives/.

Stieber, Alexandra. "Tal Ben-Shahar, Positive Psychology Expert." Wunderman Thompson Intelligence. September 01, 2015. Accessed March 02, 2020. https://intelligence.wundermanthompson.com/2012/10/qa-tal-ben-shahar-positive-psychology-expert/.

Suttie, Jill. "How to Overcome Your Brain's Fixation on Bad Things." *Greater Good Magazine.* Accessed April 22, 2020. https://greatergood.berkeley.edu/article/item/how_to_overcome_your_brains_fixation_on_bad_things.

Walker, Gordon J., Douglas A. Kleiber and Roger C. Mannell. *A Social Psychology of Leisure.* Urbana, IL: Sagamore-Venture, 2019.

Walker, Matthew P. *Why We Sleep: Unlocking the Power of Sleep and Dreams.* New York, NY: Scribner, an Imprint of Simon & Schuster, 2018.

Zawadzki, M. J., J. M. Smyth and H. J. Costigan. "Real-Time Associations Between Engaging in Leisure and Daily Health and Well-Being." *Annals of Behavioral Medicine.* (2015)

49(4), 605–615. Accessed April 29, 2020. https://doi. org/10.1007/s12160-015-9694-3.

CPSIA information can be obtained
at www.ICGtesting.com
Printed in the USA
LVHW082349141220
674195LV00057B/1998